Teaching Palahniuk

The Treasures of Transgression in the Age of Trump and Beyond

Edited by
Christopher Burlingame
Mount Aloysius College

Series in Literary Studies

Copyright © 2022 by the Authors.

All rights reserved. No part of this publication may be reproduced, stored in a retrieval system, or transmitted in any form or by any means, electronic, mechanical, photocopying, recording, or otherwise, without the prior permission of Vernon Art and Science Inc.

www.vernonpress.com

In the Americas:
Vernon Press
1000 N West Street, Suite 1200
Wilmington, Delaware, 19801
United States

In the rest of the world:
Vernon Press
C/Sancti Espiritu 17,
Malaga, 29006
Spain

Series in Literary Studies

Library of Congress Control Number: 2022930201

ISBN: 978-1-64889-456-5

Also available: 978-1-64889-281-3 [Hardback]; 978-1-64889-412-1 [PDF, E-Book]

Cover design by Vernon Press. Cover image designed by starline / Freepik.

Product and company names mentioned in this work are the trademarks of their respective owners. While every care has been taken in preparing this work, neither the authors nor Vernon Art and Science Inc. may be held responsible for any loss or damage caused or alleged to be caused directly or indirectly by the information contained in it.

Every effort has been made to trace all copyright holders, but if any have been inadvertently overlooked the publisher will be pleased to include any necessary credits in any subsequent reprint or edition.

Table of contents

Introduction: Trash, Treasure, Transgression and Teaching Chuck Palahniuk   v

Christopher Burlingame
Mount Aloysius College

Chapter 1   **Making it New: Teaching Multimedia Research through the Man-i-Verse**   1

Christopher Burlingame
Mount Aloysius College

Chapter 2   **Brodentity: Teaching Masculinity through Fight Club**   17

Jeff Ambrose
Indiana University of Pennsylvania

Chapter 3   **Teaching Creative Writing, Literary Theory, and Critical Race Theory with Palahniuk**   31

Nicole Lowman
State University of New York

Chapter 4   **"Another obsolete truth": Narrative and Construct in Chuck Palahniuk's *Rant***   49

Rebecca Warshofsky
State University of New York

Chapter 5   **The Laughter of the Dead: Theorizing Noise, Trauma, and Incantation in Palahniuk's *Lullaby***   69

Josh Grant-Young
University of Guelph

Chapter 6   **Gut-Check: The Risks of Defining and Re-Defining Capital "L" Literature as an Adjunct**   87

Christopher Burlingame
Mount Aloysius College

Chapter 7	**Cassie Wright, Stormy Daniels, and #MeToo: Teaching Chuck Palahniuk's *Snuff* as a Response to Heteropatriarchy**	103
	David McCracken *Coker University*	
Chapter 8	**The United States of Caucasia: Teaching Palahniuk in the Classroom to Raise Awareness of the Dangers of White Anxiety in America**	125
	Andrew Burlingame *Catholic University*	
	Index	*143*

Introduction: Trash, Treasure, Transgression and Teaching Chuck Palahniuk

Christopher Burlingame

Mount Aloysius College

It started in a small session at the 2018 Northeast Modern Languages Association (NeMLA) Convention in Pittsburgh. I showed up to present on a roundtable titled "Chuck Palahniuk: Literature or Trash" in the dreaded Sunday, 8:30 a.m. timeslot. I wasn't expecting much, maybe a few hung over stragglers and a couple of Palahniuk fanboys and fangirls, but I left stimulated and energized by the possibilities of everything I had not considered or expected.

After saying goodbye to a few friends who had come in for the conference, I couldn't bring myself to stop thinking about the session and my co-presenters. So, before I headed out to my car for the drive home, I claimed a small table in the lobby of the Omni William Penn Hotel and pulled out my laptop. I fired off an email to the roundtable's chair, Eyal Handelsman (now Handelsman Katz) and thanked him for the session. I asked if he'd be interested in working with me to put together a book proposal.

We started a general proposal that summer about the "treasure" rather than the "trash" of Palahniuk's work and divided the proposed books into three sections. We found the most compelling section was actually about teaching and revised the proposal to explore that underrepresented vein of research and scholarship. We didn't have enough chapters to support an edited collection, and this led to another Sunday, 8:30 a.m. session at NeMLA in 2019 titled, "Teaching Chuck Palahniuk in the Age of Trump." Eyal couldn't make the conference, and the session got re-located late Saturday night, so the panelists read to each other and an empty room. But, again, I left energized after seeing Palahniuk in a new light and understanding that his work could fulfill so many pedagogical purposes in so many different contexts.

While the impetus to create a book and share ideas rose out of part fandom, part academic interest, and part not-knowing-any-better, my recognition of the implication for using Palahniuk's work in the college and university classroom came from a more practical place. I work as a writing consultant and study skills specialist at a small liberal arts college in rural Pennsylvania.

We serve many working-class non-traditional and first-generation students, many of whom I meet with, at least initially, because they're required to bring me their first assignment in Rhetoric I, our first-year writing class. That assignment is a literacy narrative where the students are tasked with writing about their development as readers and writers. It was from reading hundreds of these narratives that I confirmed a disturbing and widespread trend among both traditional and non-traditional students: their educational experiences have made them think they *hate* reading and writing.

Many of these narratives described overly harsh teachers foisting dry, boring, and dense canon literature upon them and then telling them that they were wrong or didn't understand "the deeper meaning." The students described feeling like the beaten dead horse many of them did not actually make it to when they were assigned *Crime and Punishment*. Many described literature itself as kind of dead and lifeless and suggested that it was made more so because of how it was taught to them. Many described how the English class had made them feel dumb or "less than" because they didn't recognize *Old Man and the Sea* as a crucifixion narrative or they didn't know all the ways T.S. Eliot was alluding to ancient Greece when they were made to read *The Wasteland*. Many described how being forced to read Shakespeare crushed their spirits and how the red ink that made their essay bleed only led them to conclude that they were "no good and never would be good" at writing.

While critics of Palahniuk's work look down their nose at both his writing and his readers, with Sandra Newman writing in *The Guardian* that, "He's the sort of author who's admired by people who usually don't care for literature and scorned by people who do," his regular bestseller status and devoted fanbase suggest there is something of value in his ability to make loyal readers of those "who do not usually read fiction—and who may not read anything at all" (Keesey 3). It is this same brand of institutionalized elitism about what literature is, who writes it, who reads it, and how to teach it that was actually killing the desire to learn and read among the students I encountered. The irony is that those in academia and in the culture industries, who remain beholden to this antiquated idea of literature, literary studies and preserving tradition, are likely contributing to the crises of under-enrollment in humanities departments that result in downsizing or eliminating departments. It is arguable their own actions and approaches that provoke the need for seemingly seasonal op-eds and commentary pieces in outlets ranging from *The Chronicle* to *The Wall Street Journal* about both the death of the humanities and the dumbing down of the average citizen.

By teaching, especially literature and writing, in a way that alienates students, not only are these traditionalists endangering their present positions but also the future of their fields, more generally speaking. To go one step further, this approach empowers those, especially on the Right, who attempt to devalue frivolous educational pursuits, like an English degree, by making it a culture war issue because they recognize the potential for more easily manipulating and exploiting those who do not possess the information or literacy skills necessary to suss out political propaganda. A dangerous consequence of this long-standing political tactic seems to have become realized in the age of Trump and beyond with hyper-polarization, alternative facts, and conspiracy theories outweighing what many would have once referred as observable facts and consensus reality, especially because many of the caricatures of Palahniuk fans line up with the attempts to paint Trump fans and the Capitol rioters as what Keesey notes as "'disenfranchised Everymen'…or 'fan boys, wild with rage, choked by love and loyalty (like Ayn Rand devotees but with tattoos and tire irons)'" (5). Even more ironic, Palahniuk's 2018 novel, *Adjustment Day*, seems to predict and pre-empt the Capitol insurrection, a topic discussed in the final chapter of this collection.

This may sound a bit sensationalist, but that is only appropriate when shifting the focus to an author who so many find easy to hate. Particularly, this volume will address ways in which Palahniuk's work could be employed to innovate everything from first-year and general education courses to advanced seminars. This volume provides examples for how to teach Palahniuk across the curriculum and offers suggestions for how it could promote the kind of critical thinking that will enable a new generation of teachers, readers, and learners to better engage students with nuance and have the potential to think more independently.

While much has been written about Palahniuk, his stylistic tics and experiments, the diminished quality of his later works, and his relationship to transgressive fiction and other postmodern literary movements, little has been written about how to actually teach his works and why teaching Palahniuk is necessary and invaluable. As mentioned above, my personal motivation in pushing forward with this collection came from recognizing a problem of disinterest and lacking motivation that I think Palahniuk's work could be essential in repairing. But, beyond studying the works themselves, I view Palahniuk's work as a kind of gateway to getting students to become more invested in their own learning by granting them access to engaging plots, characters, and ideas that are rendered in language that does not seem insurmountable but familiar and even humorous. In writing about his notorious story, "Guts," Palahniuk said, "My way of handling things is to reframe the painful and uncomfortable things and turn them into stories and make them funny" (Keesey 109).

Each chapter of this collection looks at a different context in which Palahniuk's work can be employed and to what ends. The first three chapters deal with new and exciting ways Palahniuk's most taught, talked about and written about novel, *Fight Club*, can be used to achieve different pedagogical aims while the remaining five chapters address works outside of the early career sweet spot that has received the most critical praise and scholarly ink in works like Francisco Collado-Rodriguez' 2013 *Chuck Palahniuk: Fight Club, Invisible Monsters, Choke*. Because Palahniuk publishes a new book-length work almost every year, he should be considered a prolific American writer whose oeuvre demands constant re-visiting and updating of the scholarship about it. Even as I am writing this introduction, I am aware of the way my own chapter about what I call the *Fight Club* man-i-verse is in need of updating to account for the *Fight Club 3* graphic novel. Furthermore, while Palahniuk's potential to experiment with form, genre, and style is viewed by some as a weak point or failure, on his part, as a writer, it actually yields plenty of opportunities to integrate it into classrooms and onto syllabi, even in places where one might not expect it to fit.

Although my primary role at my institution is as academic staff, my experience as staff informs my work as an adjunct, and I have used Palahniuk's work in developmental courses, general education and introductory courses, and in upper-level creative writing and literature courses and seminars. What I've found in nearly ten years of teaching at the college level is that there is really not a time where something from Palahniuk's extensive oeuvre doesn't have the potential to promote or enhance student learning. I've also recognized the stigma surrounding Palahniuk's work, that comes from its perception as being both misogynist and sub-literary or unworthy, may inhibit one's decision to include his work. Using Palahniuk's work, especially in an environment that is more conservative or hostile to transgressive ideas, may actually endanger one's ability to continue teaching at a particular institution. Those who intend to employ and assign Palahniuk need to anticipate and be prepared to handle any potential resistance from students, other faculty, and administration; however, I hope that scholarship like the chapters found in this collection may be useful in validating and justifying his inclusion on syllabi.

In chapter one of this volume, I describe how the conceptualization of the *Fight Club* man-i-verse, a term I coined to describe the multimedia network over which the *Fight Club* story unfolds that includes the original novel and film adaptation, the video game, the graphic novel sequel (now two graphic novel sequels), a short story prequel, and wealth of scholarly literature, make it ideal for teaching students how to formulate and execute original, researched-based academic arguments. Situating and exploring the man-i-verse in an introduction to literature, general education course, and making a multi-step research process the culminating activity gave me the opportunity to address many of the skills with which students at my institution struggled and would need en route to graduation as they prepared to write capstone papers. My chapter draws anecdotal evidence from working as a professional writing tutor with more than seven years of experience (at that point) and now, more than 15,000 individual tutoring sessions to justify my approach. In addition, I support my tactics by referencing the work of leading educational scholars like Ken Bain, James Lang, John Warner, and others as well as citing literary criticism and scholarship from Kathryn Hume, David McCracken, Douglas Keesey, Robin Mookerjee, and others. In the chapter, I also discuss student submissions and outcomes, and I offer a brief reflection on how the project has evolved to a fully digitized model and why I shifted the project away from the man-i-verse to the one created by Margaret Atwood with *The Handmaid's Tale* in order to teach an Honors section of the same class and how I might be going back to the man-i-verse in the future.

While the first chapter is dependent upon the coining of the term man-i-verse, in chapter two, Jeff Ambrose describes how coining the term *Brodentity* has enabled him to work with students in dissecting toxic masculinity and male fragility in his course. A major challenge in teaching Palahniuk is dispelling any preconceived notion that he is a misogynist whose works advocates misogyny. For Ambrose, brodentity is the intersection and culmination of many different concepts relating to masculinity and the way it interfaces with and is reinforced by advertising, especially commercials targeted at male audiences like those from SportsClips and Nugenix. Through these advertisements that can still be found on *YouTube*, the idea of male identity and more specifically brodentity as being predicated on being sport- and sex-crazed, Bob from *Fight Club* becomes an essential character for evaluation, straying from the typical scholarly analyses of the unnamed narrator and his alter-ego, Tyler Durden. Also in this chapter, Ambrose and his students consider brodentity as it is presented in the sketch comedy of *Key & Peele* in the context of *Fight Club*, #Gamergate, and *Mulan*. He concludes his discussion of teaching about brodentity with a look at "space monkeys" from Project Mayhem and the power of images to "control, manipulate, and inform" conceptions of male identity.

Chapter three serves as the concluding perspective on *Fight Club*, and offers different ways to teach it in creative writing versus literary theory and looks ahead to how a more recent entry in the Palahniuk oeuvre, *Adjustment Day* can serve as an extension of what *Fight Club* has to offer while also serving as an opportunity to introduce Critical Race Theory. Nicole Lowman considers the role of the college teacher and the student-as-consumer model that seems to have become normalized in higher education. From the beginning, Lowman explains how the accessibility of Palahniuk's work may make it the ideal vehicle for fostering critical thinking and "achieving other curricular goals" while simultaneously providing students with material that engages them in a way more akin to general entertainment rather than dense intellectualism. For Lowman and her students, it does not have to be either entertainment or learning scenario because, with Palahniuk, one begets the next. Through sharing student journals, Lowman enters into describing how to use "Fight Club," the short story and chapter six of the novel, to provide students with a "masterclass" in character development, narrative point of view, fictional time, and figurative language. Lowman describes how her class builds up to "Fight Club" and how it is later used in creating a rubric for evaluating their mid-term short stories and short fiction, more generally. From there, Lowman addresses how *Fight Club*, the novel, can be used in a literary theory class to discuss the fundamentals of Freud's psychoanalytic theory, specifically focusing on her students' reaction to the multiple mentions of dildos, what they mean, and unpacking student reactions to the humor implicit in their appearances in the novel. The chapter concludes with Lowman highlighting the potential to expand what Palahniuk began in *Fight Club* to teaching Critical Race Theory using 2018's *Adjustment Day*. Considering that Critical Race Theory has become a hot-button issue with President Donald Trump signing an executive order banning its teaching and President Joe Biden promptly reversing that executive order, this would be a particularly timely application of a Palahniuk novel. It is yet another way that Palahniuk's work could be used to broach difficult topics with students who may be hesitant or resistant to engaging with controversial or uncomfortable subject matter.

In the fourth chapter, Rebecca Warshofsky examines and reflects on using *Rant: An Oral History of Buster Casey* with students to deconstruct norms established by the dominant culture. With *Rant*, Warshofsky and her students delve into how social norms come to exist and are often passively accepted without considering why they exist or who they serve. After a brief discussion of how Palahniuk's oeuvre, and more specifically, *Rant*, can be categorized as transgressive fiction according to frameworks provided by M. Keith Booker, Warshofsky describes how *Rant* and its cast of characters led her students to being able to re-examine "truths" that they have taken for granted. The first truth to be re-evaluated is how history and facts are actually man-made narratives that are constructed in such a way that conflicts or incongruities occur, and this can be illustrated by the inconsistencies in the narration of the multiple characters contributing to the novel's oral history framework. Furthermore, Warshofksy and her students pay special attention to the characters' treatment of how myths and myth-making of children's fairy tale figures like Santa Claus, the Easter Bunny, and Tooth Fairy are used to imbue in children a firm commitment to consumer capitalist values and what Rant, the character, and his friends do to subvert the capitalist system and its implicit promotion of values that perpetuate the system. Another instance of

Palahniuk's characters transgressing socially-constructed norms that are "surreptitiously motivated by the value of consumerism" is how they co-opt the roadways and traffic system with "Party Crashing" and later, time, itself, with "Boosting Peaks." Throughout her chapter, Warshofsky cites student work and notes critical texts that are essential to frame her use of *Rant* to help students improve critical thinking in such a way that they are better prepared to "trace the lineage of a narrative through power by demonstrating the point at which that power breaks down." Warshofsky concludes that Palahniuk's *Rant*, and transgressive fiction, more broadly, could provide students, as members of society, with the tools necessary to promote potentially revolutionary changes to the status quo.

In his chapter five discussion of Palahniuk's *Lullaby*, Josh Grant-Young not only challenges conventional critical approaches to Palahniuk's work as social critique, but he offers opportunities for how students can engage with a more nuanced and multi-faceted response to the novel by considering it in the context of Trauma narratives. Grant-Young defines trauma and trauma narratives and suggests students analyze the anti-hero, Carl Streator's, behavior as a traumatic response rather than a simple critique of "our media-inundated culture." Grant-Young provides a brief discussion of the Gothic Loop and its role in horror as a genre and its prevalence in trauma narratives due to its role in Post-Traumatic Stress Disorder as it relates to sound being a triggering device. In the wake of trauma being perpetuated by the Gothic Loop, Grant-Young argues for how this can lead to narrative unreliability, which reinforces the premise that *Lullaby*'s protagonist is not simply critiquing society but reacting to the way it re-traumatizes him. While noise, which includes the narrative itself, is central to traumatizing Streator, Grant-Young offers both the readers and his students an analysis of the way lullabies attempt to control noise and trauma by serving as a kind of "reparative sound" and how the very premise of Palahniuk's *Lullaby* is to acknowledge the destructive potential behind this gesture. By transgressing the predominant response to Palahniuk's work as social critique Grant-Young suggests students are better able to understand the importance of both noise and silence in the novel and beyond.

My chapter six about teaching the short story, "Guts," is a post-mortem reflection on the experience of teaching, and continuing to teach, a story that provokes visceral responses such as nausea and fainting. However, I also explore how the tenuous position of an increasingly adjunctified faculty may result in valuable, controversial works like "Guts" being left off syllabi and how this could inhibit the full potential of student engagement and learning. The chapter opens with the horror and anxiety I experienced in preparing to teach "Guts" in my creative writing class. It had been more than 10 years since I read it, but I included it on my own syllabus because of the mythos surrounding people reportedly fainting when Palahniuk read the story aloud at his promotional events. Because I teach as an adjunct at a small, Catholic liberal arts college in a rural and conservative region of central Pennsylvania, re-reading the story made me literally fear for my job because all that needs to happen for me to lose 'the privilege' of being able to teach as an adjunct in addition to my full-time academic staff position is for one student to complain to administration. As I re-read the descriptions of explicit self-mutilations that resulted from the different character's masturbatory pursuits, I realized that the lines of what one can and cannot or should and should not include, even if it provokes actual deep learning among students through discussion and the writing that results, are very different for those protected by tenure and those, like myself, who are not. I trace not only the discussion from that night, which was so intensive and informed by re-visiting the Palahniuk essay, "Not Chasing Amy," that we'd read earlier in the semester, that even in our nearly three-hour class, we did not get to any of the other assigned readings that night. But I also address why I now regularly teach the story as a part of my Honors section of Rhetoric II, our introduction to literature course in our general education requirements. Throughout the chapter, I justify my use of the story by citing critical scholarship from Keesey and McCracken as well as research on Higher Education trends and pedagogy from writers like James Lang and Rebecca Recco. The chapter is as much a deep-dive on "Guts" and teaching it as a model for creative writers as it is about the vulnerability of adjunct labor and how that vulnerability could endanger the richness of student learning.

The final two chapters consider novels that enable the authors to handle "ripped from the headlines" current events by looking back to Palahniuk novels that seem to anticipate the events with great prescience. In the seventh chapter, David McCracken addresses his most successful instance of using 2008's *Snuff* to contextualize the #MeToo movement and Stormy Daniels' exchange with President Trump in his 2019 special topics class on Dirty Realism. McCracken opens with discussion of Alyssa Milano and Waleisah Wilson's CNN op-ed calling for a #SexStrike that aligns with one represented in Aristophanes' *Lysistrata*. Much like my own experience with "Guts," McCracken acknowledges that *Snuff*, a novel about the porn industry and a 600-man gangbang that ends in multiple deaths, is not for timid instructors. He suggests that it took him three times to ensure the appropriate framing with feminist theorists for it to have his desired effect with students at his small, Southern university. In addition to having students read works by Andrea Dworkin, Ariel Levy and Sheila Jeffreys, McCracken's students are eased into *Snuff* after reading stories from the collection *Make Something Up: Stories You Can't Unread*. McCracken guided his students through considering

Introduction   xiii

the role of power and heteropatriarchy in sexual interactions, and this is where the Stormy Daniels/President Trump revelation, the feminist theorists and *Snuff* intersected. With the groundwork laid, McCracken asks his students to hold back their prejudices about sex and pornography as they read and discuss *Snuff*. When teaching such a potentially controversial novel, McCracken is clear about the necessity of providing students with extensive critical preparation because it enables most to consider something beyond the initial spectacle of sex and sexuality. In particular, McCracken's students tackled three key questions while synthesizing the novel with the critical theorists and the #MeToo Movement and Stormy Daniels affair: 1. Was Cassie Wright raped? 2. Is Cassie manipulated into participating in the gangbang? 3. Is Cassie redeemed at the novel's end? McCracken describes how he and his students work through these questions and highlights how 2008's *Snuff* still holds up more than ten years later because heteropatriarchal power and toxic masculinity still have yet to be resolved.

The final entry in this collection is a historical perspective on using *Adjustment Day* to help students understand and trace the deep roots of white anxiety in the American social consciousness. Andrew Burlingame opens with an epigraph of side-by-side quotations from both Donald Trump and Benjamin Franklin that seem to echo one another in their vilification of an immigrating other. While some attribute the January 6, 2021 siege on the Capitol as being a culmination of Trump's persistent stoking of nationalist, white identity politics, history has painted a rosier picture of Franklin as a kind of benevolent founding father. However, after showing some of the parallels between the coup in *Adjustment Day* and the January 6, 2021 insurrection at the Capitol, Burlingame illustrates the "long history of racism, nativism, religious intolerance, and the persecution and scapegoating of the 'other' by the dominant white class in America." Burlingame suggests looking at the contemporary rise of white nationalism, and the call by leaders of the alt-right, like Richard Spencer, to form an ethno-state, are critiqued and mocked by Palahniuk in *Adjustment Day* with Caucasia devolving into chaos. Burlingame shows, generation-by-generation, dating from the colonial period to the present, how the once marginalized group will adopt the tactics of their oppressors in order to assimilate and be considered white Americans, while the dominant white class will only accept the formerly scapegoated "other" once a new "other" poses a greater risk to the illusion of a white American identity to which they cling. Palahniuk is quick to point out the flimsiness of this approach, and Burlingame suggests how fiction, like *Adjustment Day*, may fit well in history and political science classes due to its potential for disarming student apprehension to any historical narrative and evidence that seeks to revise or complicate the narrative of American progress and exceptionalism in which most of them have been educated. The students may say, "it's just fiction," so they'll be less likely to grow defensive; however, Burlingame argues that the absurdity of the white ethno-state of Caucasia in *Adjustment Day* may serve as a bridge to getting students to more fully consider the historical implications of white anxiety and nativism as well as the current danger they pose in a post-Trump-presidency America that cannot seem to free itself from the ideas he purported, in part because, like his slogan, "Make America Great Again," it was all plagiarized from the bigots that came before him.

This collection owes a great deal of gratitude to Eyal Handelsman Katz for organizing the first NeMLA roundtable and to the teachers and scholars in the collection who are finding innovative ways to bring the validation to Palahniuk's work that it deserves by making it a necessary part of the academic discourse. Palahniuk will continue to publish and experiment by pushing boundaries of form and content, and teachers need to be ready to promote student engagement and learning by bringing them into the fold. One point that working on this collection has led me to realize is that with the works beyond the critically acclaimed big three—*Fight Club, Choke,* and *Invisible Monsters*—Palahniuk is being punished for his attempts to innovate, and this criticism of his imitations of literary forms and experiments with genre seems antithetical to the creation of unique art. A common trope in the literary critics' responses to his work is to fixate on the spectacle and refer to Palahniuk's writing as misogynistic, sophomoric and sub-literary, but what seems to have been overlooked and demands to be incorporated into classrooms around the world is his deep knowledge of and deference to literary traditions. If his readers are the type of people who don't usually read or value literature, isn't a work like *Haunted,* which is structured like classic works of literature like *The Decameron* and *The Canterbury Tales,* not a gateway for these mouth-breathing heathens to find their way to "L" Literature? Aren't works like *Snuff* or *Adjustment Day* or *Rant* a great way for people who may have been conditioned to not question hetero-patriarchal consumer capitalism an opportunity to re-assess their own values and their role in society? As a nation, we cannot claim to value freedom, liberty, justice and critical thinking but not champion works that help people develop the skills and agency to exercise those values. While Palahniuk may not be a part of the canon, he should be. It is my hope, and the hope of this collection's contributors, that we are only scratching the surface of how Palahniuk's oeuvre can find its ways into contributing to the learning and diversification of ideas in higher education.

Chapter 1

Making it New: Teaching Multimedia Research through the Man-i-Verse

Christopher Burlingame

Mount Aloysius College

Abstract: Working at small liberal arts college with a large population of students enrolled in professional programs like nursing, medical imaging, and criminology, a constant challenge faced in general education courses like Rhetoric II (Introduction to Literature) is resistance from students who do not see the value of being made to take these courses. When given the opportunity to teach Rhetoric II, I joined together my personal and academic interests in Chuck Palahniuk and my awareness of the student needs in developing research and writing skills to graduate in an ever-evolving market. In 2015 and 2016, Palahniuk's release of the short story, "Expedition," and a graphic novel sequel, *Fight Club 2*, expanded the *Fight Club* man-i-verse and created new footholds for scholars attempting to enter the academic discourse around his most researched work. Because the man-i-verse spans so many different media, it poses both a challenge and a rich opportunity, especially for a novice researcher, to develop the skills necessary to be able to approach, formulate and execute an original claim, something that is in-demand across all disciplines. By making my culminating project for Rhetoric II an open-ended research assignment where students have to survey the extant literature and formulate a new, original argument on the *Fight Club* man-i-verse, I have found a way to help them gain a deeper appreciation of literature by using it as a scaffolding from which they can leap into the academic discourse and come out with transferable skills.

Keywords: Fight Club, Chuck Palahniuk, Man-i-Verse, Research, Multimedia

***

They stood waiting, three-in-a-row, each holding a single sheet of copy paper. Without a word, the first student handed me her paper. Below the MLA heading where the title should have been it said, "The first rule of fight club is you don't talk about fight club." She stepped aside, and the student behind her stepped forward extending a nearly identical single leaf of paper, "The second rule of fight club is you don't talk about fight club." She sidestepped, making way for the final student to hand me a last single sheet that said, "Only two men per fight." The three students did an about-face, returned to their single-file line and began to march back to their seats. They burst out laughing. The first woman, a nursing student—they were all nursing students—turned and said, "Sorry, we couldn't keep it together." They went back to their computers to get their actual research papers.

It was the final night of my Rhetoric II class in December 2018. At my institution, the name is misleading. Rhetoric II is actually the Introduction to Literature course in the general education sequence of core classes. I should pause to mention two things that will be significant to understanding what this is all about: 1. I work at a school that operates under the moniker of being a liberal arts college; however, our bread and butter are actually professional programs like criminology, nursing and medical imaging, meaning that in order to accommodate their clinical schedules, many of these students have to take their general education credits in the evening after spending a whole day at clinical, leading to very tired and sometimes, understandably disengaged students and 2. I am a professional writing tutor, by day, who works with students from across the curriculum, averaging more than 1,500 sessions per year, and an adjunct instructor, by night, who normally is given the developmental writing and first-year composition students. I hold an MFA in fiction writing, and I have since completed a Ph.D. in literature and criticism with a dissertation on adapting transgressive fiction. So, when I get the chance to teach literature, I treat it as a real opportunity to take my teaching to the next level by bringing in work that I love and finding new ways to challenge students who may not have a real interest or even see a need to take a class like the ones I most often teach.

As Douglas Keesey notes, Chuck Palahniuk "connects with working-class people, many of them young, who do not usually read fiction—and who may not regularly read anything at all. His writing features characters, situations, and language with which they can identify" (3). While this is true, and factored into my decision to include *Fight Club* on my syllabus, there is actually a bigger factor that I am calling the *Fight Club* man-i-verse. Similar to the increasing number of multi-verses or cinematic universes, like Marvel or DC or *Star Wars*, Palahniuk has created a world of characters that cross so many forms of media, with which students can engage, that include a short story, a novel, a film, two graphic novels, a video game, a wealth of scholarship, and has become a kind of "cultural meme" where individuals may know of *Fight Club* and are able to reference things like the rules without even knowing from where these references come (Keesey 3). Furthermore, it is hard to separate *Fight Club* and its extended universe from understandings and misunderstanding regarding how he portrays masculinity when Palahniuk, himself, notes in "There was a Book," (an introduction in my edition of *Fight Club* that appears as an afterword in other editions), "there was no novel that presented a new social model for men to share their lives" (xvi). The man-i-verse is complex and bears being examined piece-by-piece for how it was addressed in my discussion of it as a whole and for how it led to the creation of unique student research.

Developing and Implementing the Man-i-Verse into the Curriculum

But first, I think I should address how I found a place for the man-i-verse. As our college's writing tutor, it became apparent that our students were really struggling with the process of conducting and executing original research, a point further confirmed by the director of our capstone program. He held his office hours next to my desk in the library. He encouraged me to experiment. In particular, he pointed out that, even after being engaged in college writing for four years, our students had difficulty with academic articles. They had trouble prioritizing and incorporating relevant, academically appropriate sources just as much as they were not sure how to synthesize non-traditional sources and various forms of media to respond to and develop original claims. Many of our professional programs are more geared toward informational rather than argumentative writing; however, all students had to produce an original, argumentative 20-page research paper as a capstone. This research had to address a current issue pertinent to their field of study and also had to be able to be linked to the Mercy Values of the order of nuns responsible for founding our institution, the Sisters of Mercy, which are service, justice, hospitality and mercy, as well as acknowledge the implications to at least two other liberal arts disciplines. The 20-page requirement alone is enough to give our students pause; however, most founder when it comes to being current with emerging issues in their field because their training, coursework and clinical work is more about staying in the moment of the challenge directly in front of them. While this may seem like a criticism, I only intend to provide context, drawn from more than 15,000 student appointments, about why our students enter their capstone experience feeling underprepared and how I sought to pilot a plan to remedy the issue. Because Rhetoric II is a course required of both our associate's and bachelor's students, it was the perfect point of contact to entertain my experiment with the *Fight Club* man-i-verse as a route to enhancing the students' multimedia research competencies. When I got my fall course schedule in March 2018, it was three years since I had last been given the opportunity to teach a literature course, so I was already anticipating balancing my class' reading list between canon and non-canon works that would better engage my evening students. Also, in the fall of 2018, I was writing and defending my comprehensive doctoral exams, which included my own extended discussion of what I'd been calling the *Fight Club* man-i-verse. I should mention too that the capstone director was not only a professor in our English department, but as a member of my dissertation committee, he was familiar with and central to my conceiving of the man-i-verse and its pedagogical implications.

It wasn't exactly a light bulb moment, but this fictional world of Tyler Durden and the unnamed narrator had everything students might want to use to conduct 21st century research, and so, I designed the course to culminate with a project that challenged them to read, watch, or play everything in the man-i-verse and study the extant literature to formulate their own new and original argument in very active and lively discourse. Although published after I developed this class, I was, in effect, trying to turn my Rhetoric II into what Ken Bain would call a "Super Course" for the way it would foster "deeper and more widespread learning" by redefining "what it means to become educated and the conditions most likely to produce that end" (3). I ordered the video game through eBay and dug out and cleaned off my PlayStation 2 so I could have it available for anyone who wanted to play the game. My number one goal was giving the students skills that could be transferred to courses within their respective disciplines and, more specifically, to conducting their capstone research project. But, beyond that, I wanted to expand their concept of what they could view as worthy subject matter for conducting original research. Here is the language I included in my assignment sheet in Canvas, our learning management system:

> Our entire semester has led us to this point and this paper. Let's break the first rule together!
>
> For this assignment, you will be doing a deep dive to provide a unique take on the *Fight Club* man-i-verse. You are responsible for reviewing the extant literature so that you can propose and execute an original argument. Although you won't always be writing only about *Fight Club*, the processes we'll be working through are analogous to any form of research writing, but more specifically to writing a capstone-type research assignment. The multimedia nature of *Fight Club*, its adaptations, prequels, and sequels, as well as its extensive implications

on popular culture, make it fertile ground for the construction of new knowledge. Enter the fray and find your place.

Defining the Man-i-Verse and its Parts: The Original Short Story and Novel

Teaching the novel, let alone explaining to students that it began as a "seven-page short story" or chapter six of the novel, proved to be a bigger challenge than I anticipated because, since its 1996 publication and the 1999 film adaptation, not only were students unfamiliar with it being a book but most had never seen or heard of the film (Palahniuk xvi). This marked the first time in my teaching that I felt self-conscious about being old—I was 32. For me, reading *Fight Club* has been essential to my growth as a reader, writer, and thinker. My first encounter with it came when my co-worker and fellow high school student, another lifeguard at the local university's indoor pool, left it for me to read during the many down times of my shift. My first exposure was all-consuming: I read it in an afternoon; I watched the film adaptation; I raved about it to others and shared my copy freely; I rounded up and read all of Palahniuk's other published works; and as I developed as a creative writer, I experimented with stylistics that were characteristic of Palahniuk's work. It seemed so foreign to me that none of my students were consciously familiar with it. I later realized only two of my students had even been born as of 1996. They were aware, like the cowboy guide on the Haunted Tunnel Tour from Palahniuk's Introduction/Afterward, of the rules without being aware of their source, and I wanted them to not only appreciate the book, but where it started and how it expanded, both with and without Palahniuk's input.

Because of my own creative writing background, an essential part of my teaching literature is helping students understand the creative process and the genesis of works. Earlier in the semester, I had had my students understand storytelling by experimenting with writing a story of their own, and then we used that experience to discuss how this whole novel, and later, man-i-verse, could coalesce from a seven-page short story. We spent a great deal of our dissection of the novel by charting how much of the overall plot can be found or at least hinted at in chapter six. We talked about the shifting point of view from "I" to "you" in the narration. We talked about the rules as a structural and organizational device. We talked about the ideas about masculinity like the line, "What you see in fight club is a generation of men raised by women" or nihilist philosophical perspectives like "maybe we have to break everything to make something better out of ourselves" (Palahniuk 41; 43). We talked about descriptive language like "broken noses spreading out like an eggplant under the edges of bandages" and how to shift through time by framing the story with the narrator weaving in and out of running a slideshow presentation during a business meeting. Many of our revelations about what we'd later come to refer to as "the source," came from a deep dive into chapter six and everything for which it lays the foundation in the rest of the novel and in the film adaptation as well as everything that would come after, and is still coming.

The Film

One of the advantages of my contingent role is that I am not allowed to teach during the regular 8:30 to 5 p.m. workday. While this may seem inconvenient, it means that rather than teaching courses that meet either two or three days a week for 45 minutes or 65 minutes, I get my students one night a week for two hours and 50 minutes. This means that we were able to watch the entire film together in one sitting. In the pre-COVID world, I made and passed out popcorn to all of the students and spent as much time watching their reactions to the film as I did to the film itself. Grimaces. Laughter. Confused expressions and exchanged whispers. Also, it wasn't until the film began that it fully dawned on me that I had only one male student in a class that was watching a film that has quite a great deal to say about masculinity and its problems (even if more than a few critics and lay viewers have mistaken it as an endorsement or glorification of toxic masculinity).

When the film wrapped, we didn't have time for a full discussion; instead, we came back together to generate some focus questions that would be used frame our class the next week when we'd also be discussing the graphic novel sequel, *Fight Club 2: The Tranquility Gambit* and the short story prequel, "Expedition," from the collection *Make Something Up: Stories You Can't Unread*. Students were immediately interested in discussing the different ending in David Fincher's film, and as a fan of the whole man-i-verse, I had to exercise some self-control in not immediately indulging their energized investment in opening this topic of discussion. We all had places to be, and it was apparent that this was not going to be resolved quickly by any of us. The answer to the question posed by the title of the song by the Pixies, "Where is my Mind?," at the end of the film and during the formulation of these focus questions, is probably best described as "already racing to the next week's class." Some other topics they were itching to discuss included the meaning of the shaking camera and spliced pornography, and one student mentioned this quote from an interview with Palahniuk she found on *DVDtalk*, "Now that I see the movie, especially when I sat down with Jim Uhls and record a commentary track for the DVD, I was sort of embarrassed of the book, because the movie had streamlined the plot and made it so much more effective and made connections that I had never thought to make" (Kleinman). Unprompted, the student had watched the film on her own time and had been searching the internet for some additional information: articles, interviews, and *YouTube* videos. This was my first hint that I was on the right track. As James Lang notes in his book, *Distracted: Why Students Can't Focus and What We Can Do About It,* "If we have lost the attention of our students, we're in trouble...[because] Teaching fails when we can no longer focus our students' attention" (4-5). So, I promised this could be our entry point the following week. The Palahniuk interview would give us the opportunity to address how the plot of the film enters into the construction of the sequel and disrupts a simple chronology in the man-i-verse.

The Sequel, Prequel, and Coming to Play (the video game)

A surprise I set up for the students when they came into class the next week was that I had the video game cued up and ready to play as well as the tables at the back of the room covered in Palahniuk paraphernalia (a signed severed plastic arm that had been hurled into the crowd at a 2015 Palahniuk reading event in Pittsburgh, all of Palahniuk's other published books, and screen-printed artwork on rice paper that my brother found in Vietnam) and my collection of scholarly articles and books about Palahniuk and his work that I'd been collecting for my comprehensive exams and in anticipation of writing my dissertation on adapting transgressive literature. I only had one taker for a fight in the very poorly made, bordering on nonsensical video game that Cassidy from *Bad Game Hall of Fame* says "is a monument to the very same corporate disinterest and greed that the novel and film sought to satirize," adding "now that the dust has settled and the corporations involved no longer stand to profit...give the story mode a look, and have a laugh at the all-singing, all-dancing crap on display." Our bout was fraught with clunky and limited moves from our fighters, and the rest of the students only paused briefly to watch as I lost. Instead, they circulated around the other tables like scavengers at a yard sale. My student put the controller down and said, "That sucked." All I could do was nod, and ask if anyone else wanted to try it out. No luck.

I let them look through the table for a little longer before asking them if they could explain why, if Palahniuk was embarrassed by his book, would he not only write a sequel, but a prequel? While *Fight Club 2* is, in part, predicated on tapping into audience nostalgia and familiarity with both the original novel and film, by revisiting characters, re-creating scenes, offering inside jokes and allusions, as well as expanding upon and complicating the Tyler/narrator (referred to as Sebastian in *Fight Club 2)* dynamic, "Expedition" is a little trickier. First of all, the story is embedded in a collection of stories that "Palahniuk has claimed...is his most transgressive," and in the story, it is not made apparent, at least initially, that there is any linkage to *Fight Club* (McCracken 125). So, the graphic novel benefits from satisfying the explicit demand for a sequel, even one a fictionalized and illustrated Palahniuk, in

Fight Club 2, acknowledges will disappoint his fans, but "Expedition" is likely designed to feel more like a discovery or Easter egg hidden, for truly devoted fans, in an unexpected place. Even though I knew when I read it that "Expedition" is a prequel in the chronology of the *Fight Club* man-i-verse, I will admit to *nerding out* as I started to see the dots connect with the mention of a modified version of the rules, "the first-most rule regarding meeting the monster is thee must nevermore speak of meeting the monster," and the later revelation that the guide who leads the story's protagonist to a face-off with his entrapped father is, in fact, Tyler. For me, "Exhibition" is both a rewarding and frustrating entry in the man-i-verse, but it is made richer by Tyler explaining Sebastian's family tree draped with limp sperm in *Fight Club 2* (Palahniuk et al. 201). Palahniuk's ability to both extend his man-i-verse and recognize and even mock his role in it is a significant factor in what prompted me to want to bring the man-i-verse into the classroom and onto the syllabus.

Although published well after I taught this class in late 2018, in his 2020 book, *Chuck Palahniuk and the Comic Grotesque: Subversion of Ideology in the Fiction*, David McCracken states, "this story ['Expedition'] traces the origin of paternal anger spanning from Felix to Sebastian in *Fight Club 2*" and notes that Felix is "[e]stablished as an ancestor of the narrator in *Fight Club*" (139-140). To be perfectly honest, most of my students, at least initially, hated "Expedition" and were only interested in circling back around to it after trying to suss out why Tyler assassinates Palahniuk at the end of *Fight Club 2*. They became very interested in the role of the author and the whole concept of meta-fiction. They wanted to talk about the legacy of the original novel versus the film and how both are alluded to and complicated by both the prequel and the sequel.

So, I let them.

I have long since abandoned the idea of coming to class with a set of notes to give, and I always request a room in the library that has a large screen and projector and sound bar, enough computers to facilitate in-class writing, and a separate space in the back of the room with moveable tables and a big-screen television mounted to the wall. I have been committed to the idea that the second chapter of David Gooblar's book, *The Missing Course: Everything They Never Taught about College Teaching*, refers to as "Letting Students Own the Course" (44). Even if sometimes I have to prime the students with a prompt or question, I like to let students guide the discussion and follow their own interests and trains of thought because as Gooblar notes, "[i]f we're always trying to steer students to our point, or if we cut off discussion after a certain amount of time because we've got something else planned, students will understand the game is rigged...But if we truly listen to students and let them change the trajectory of the class period, we can open up the classroom for students to take the lead" (53). I made sure to hold on to their anger and hatred of "Expedition" because the degree of emotional investment they expressed has often proven to be a viable source to producing original research, but I certainly did not tell my students that just yet.

Scholarship

One of the greater challenges our students face is conceiving of themselves as scholars. Too often, the rhythm of writing and submitting academic papers over the course of a semester makes it feel like an isolated incident rather than an engagement in a discursive relationship with an on-going scholarly exchange of ideas. For this reason, our students, as I assume is the same for students at numerous institutions around the world, struggle to seek out, identify and incorporate relevant secondary sources in their written work. Many of them don't know what peer review is or why their teachers care about it. Many of them don't see the problem with starting and ending their research with a simple Google search. I became increasingly aware of this reality because another facet of my role as a professional writing tutor is that I often collaborate with our college's librarians on classroom presentations about information literacy and library resources. This is a by-product of the Learning Commons being housed in and formerly under the jurisdiction of the Library; however, it is through this work that I found how little students had been educated on just what is expected of them in writing research papers, let alone how to go about preparing for and writing them.

Because Rhetoric II is most often scheduled for the second semester of the first year, I opted to use the man-i-verse and its associated scholarship because I already had so much of it on hand. As mentioned above, I spread my books and articles across the tables in the back of my classroom in the library that night. I wanted students to have tangible access to a wealth of resources. I've come to recognize that they were not quite processing what was necessary by hovering over the hyperlinks to articles in our college's databases. I wanted the students to pick up an article or a book like the obviously related edited collections like Francisco Collado-Rodriguez' *Chuck Palahniuk: Fight Club, Invisible Monsters, Choke* or books that may deal with Palahniuk like Kathryn Hume's *Aggressive Fictions: Reading the Contemporary American Novel* or Robin Mookerjee's *Transgressive Fiction: The New Satiric Tradition*. I hoped by allowing them to hold and sort through some of these works, they would become more familiar with the diverse range of scholarly resources they could employ. After our discussion of "Expedition," *Fight Club 2* and the film, I reserved time to send students back to the resources on the table and talk with each other about what they may want to write. I directed each student to one article or chapter and then walked them all through reference mining, finding additional sources from the works cited or reference lists of published works. I also explained how they could translate these processes into the digital realm as well as how to use interlibrary loan.

Finally, before I sent them on their way into the snowy mountain night, I talked a little about my on-going revision process for publishing a peer-reviewed article that would appear in the April 2019 issue of the *Journal of Popular Culture* about *American Psycho* and Donald Trump. I explained that I came across an interview in *Rolling Stone* where *American Psycho's* author, Bret Easton Ellis, made a claim about how even Patrick Bateman wouldn't have been able to vote for Donald Trump because of who Trump was appealing to in 2016. I told them that this simple comment led me to writing an article countering this claim. I walked them through the original formulation of my argument and where it fell short, how it received a split decision from the peer-reviewers, and how I had to refine my argument by incorporating social identity theory. My main focus in discussing this process was how I had to look in places I may not have expected for secondary sources and that, ultimately, being directed to Georgia Warnke's essay, "Hermeneutics and Social Identity," by a member of my dissertation committee was the breakthrough I needed to bring my argument to its final form. And, from there, I showed them how to map an argument and create keywords beyond simply searching for "Chuck Palahniuk" or "*Fight Club*".

Fruits of Our Labor

According to 2016's *Professional Knowledge for the Teaching of Writing*, which replaced 2004's *NCTE* [National Council of Teachers of English] *Beliefs about the Teaching of Writing*, "In order to provide high-quality writing opportunities for all students, teachers need to understand…ways of organizing and transforming curricula in order to provide students with adequate education in varied purposes of writing," as well as "[h]ow to set up a course that asks students to write for varied purposes and audiences." It is from this document that I set out to create assignments that would build students, step-by-step to writing an extended, research-based argument. For this end-of-semester project, I gave them more than a month to submit an annotated bibliography and proposal. From there, they turned it in to and presented an academic-conference-style paper/presentation at a mock academic conference in class. I gave them another week to revise the paper based on the questions and feedback they received from their classmates and myself. I have also gotten into the habit of including explicit learning objectives as well as a translation of what that learning objective should mean to them:

Learning Objectives: You should be able to complete the research process from developing an idea to refining the final copy.

Why it should matter to you. *Writing research-based arguments is the very crux of academic writing, but it is also a way to establish your position as a thinker, contributor, and asset beyond the classroom because it shows that you have ideas that are grounded and likely to succeed.

However, my work with students revealed their being turned off or disengaged when taking this class with faculty members who used the more conventional anthologies. To me, this demanded that I employ content that would both pique their interest and would be presented to them in a scaffolded learning environment. I wanted to get my students to first respond with pathos like the horror and revulsion that is a common reaction to the violence and *on-the-bodiness* that is characteristic of Palahniuk's work (Palahniuk, *Stranger than Fiction* 145). According to Gooblar, "The best teachers respond to students in the moment, working with them as they figure things out. They don't fear uncertainty but embrace it as a necessary precondition of learning…They leave open the possibility that they might fail" (227). I wanted to take the risk of letting them share their emotional responses and try to understand them, because I wanted them to harness that fire into an actual argument, a premise drawn from modifying a writing experience in John Warner's *The Writer's Practice* called, "Why am I so angry and what can I do about it?" (163).

Once the students identified their emotional and visceral response to watching the film in our three-hour class and discussing it in relation to the novel and later, the graphic novel sequel and the short story prequel, we brainstormed lists of all the students' kernels of anger, discussed what kind of scholarship they'd already found, and where they could use that kernel to carve out their own niche. This was my attempt to build off of *The Meaningful Writing Project* by Eodice et al. and follow James Lang's advice from his *Chronicle* article, "Will They Remember Writing It?" by "Giving the Students a Say." Students were able to use their own anger as a tactic to develop some agency in shaping a writing assignment that mattered to them. Also, because I plopped the students down in such a wide-open man-i-verse and told them to go crazy, I attempted (and I think succeeded) in achieving Lang's second step of "engaging them actively, not passively."

One student situated a discussion of masculinity in the *Fight Club* man-i-verse in the context of the rise to prominence of Jordan Peterson. The student argued about how Peterson's *YouTube* presence has elevated his status to parroting or re-packaging the ethos behind many of Tyler Durden's misguided aphorisms by using the thesis statement, "Society is the cause of detrimental results that stem from masculinity because of the promotion of violence, enhancement of materialistic value and dulling the general senses as to what gives life meaning and the pursuit of truth and happiness." In particular, the student compared Project Mayhem in *Fight Club* and Rize or Die International in *Fight Club 2* with Peterson's claim about how men need to find purpose. The student acknowledged the parallels between how Peterson has found favor among young men while also being castigated as misogynistic in much the same way Durden and *Fight Club* were upon publication and the release of the film adaptation. According to the student, "Peterson explains this in his lecture when describing the importance of truth and meaning and being fulfilled and truly successful...But meaning stems from having something valuable to oneself that cannot be measured or taken away." The argument was extremely ambitious and exceeded the page limit of the assignment by more than half as the student wrestled with the confluence of these complex ideas. I should also mention this is the same student who found the interview where Palahniuk expressed being embarrassed by the book upon seeing Jim Uhls' work as a screenwriter in the film adaptation. Throughout the process of writing the proposal, meeting with me to revise the research question and develop a thesis, the student learned to cite online videos, discussion forums of men's rights groups, peer-reviewed research and incorporate extensive close readings of the novel, the film and the graphic novel. While not a perfect argument, when the student came to pick up the paper at the end of the semester, she expressed how her project excited interest and took the project in several unexpected directions. I asked the student what provoked such an energized response, and she said it started with finding a piece of something that was already of interest and finding ways to weave that into making something new. Before we ended our session, and I returned the paper, we talked about how the student could use that same approach in writing a capstone about nursing, and this fulfilled step three, according to Lang, of "making sure it transfers" both in and out. It's about finding that little spark.

Two other students found the same interview with Chuck Palahniuk where he claims that all of his books are love stories. They carpooled to their nursing clinical site together and had been arguing about the brazen provocation implicit in this claim and how it did not jibe with Palahniuk's brutal and transgressive approach to storytelling. They came to me after we finished watching the film in class, and one wanted to follow the love story tropes and match them up with *Fight Club* while the other wanted to directly challenge all of the ways that the novel, the film and the graphic novel are antithetical to this genre. And they were off. They actually worked together to gather many of their sources about love stories and romance but put them to use in their arguments in such different ways. They argued interpretations, and I'm not ashamed to admit that much of their learning took place outside the confines of the classroom and our regular meetings. These were two of the young women who came up with the scheme to just hand in the rules of fight club and were also students who claimed to not like reading or writing, but they found they liked arguing and competing. Isn't that what academic discourse is all about, at least to some extent?

A few other takes that surprised me and were argued to varying degrees of success included a discussion about the American way of life as depicted or satirized in the *Fight Club* and *Purge* franchises, a paper in response to a reddit thread about Marla being an equally illusory figure to the narrator's Tyler Durden alter-ego, and a deep dive about how *Fight Club*, as a franchise, should be used as a teaching tool for psychologists who will be working with patients with Dissociative Identity Disorder. For these projects, students not only had to turn in proposals, but my role as a professional tutor means I have 40 available office hours each week during which I provided them with a variety of feedback beyond what they received from in-class speed dating reviews and small-group workshops. This assignment fulfills what Hassel and Giordano describe in "Occupy Writing Studies: Rethinking College Composition for the Needs of the Teaching Majority" in the way that it recognizes how Rhetoric II instructors who follow this approach "are well-positioned to develop increasingly better ways of preparing students to meet the rigorous expectations of college-level reading, writing, and thinking" (126).

Palahniuk's work, even his most commercially and critically accepted *Fight Club* man-i-verse, is challenging, unfamiliar, and outside the norm of what students expect to get from an intro to lit. course, and that's what makes it an invaluable tool for both engaging students with the literature and film as well as creating an opening for them to develop as researchers. I've come to framing my classes with an excerpt from Nick Sousanis' fantastic graphic novel-style dissertation, *Unflattening*, because it shows faceless characters trapped on conveyor belts being shifted from place to place without any agency or freedom. And, too often, what Sousanis describes as "flat" or uninspired thought leads to automation and getting stuck in prescriptive patterns that turn students away from being able to enjoy reading and writing. This is precisely what John Warner traces back to being the root cause of poor student writing in *Why They Can't Write: Killing the Five-Paragraph Essay and Other Necessities*. Palahniuk's work has a place, not just in creative writing and upper-level literature courses, but it can be an invaluable tool for unflattening student concepts of reading, writing, and how they view themselves as researchers and writers.

Beyond My First Foray into the Man-i-Verse

Since teaching this class in late 2018, I've both continued to use the project and have steered away from the man-i-verse to other fictional multi-verses. Over the past few summers, I taught a version of Rhetoric II that has been condensed to eight weeks and is fully online. For this class, which I run asynchronously, I kept the *Fight Club* man-i-verse project mostly intact. We don't get to watch the film together and the spontaneity of responses and harnessing the initial pathos of those responses is lacking for me, but students continue to respond well to all the unique multimedia facets of the man-i-verse. In my more recent opportunities to teach Rhetoric II in person, I have taken over teaching the Honors section and am now engaging with a very different set of issues in *The Handmaid's Tale* extended universe. I wanted the chance to have students tackle a television or streaming series while still dealing with a graphic novel and a sequel. I have not abandoned Palahniuk or lost faith in the pedagogical potential in using his man-i-verse, but at the time, there was a greater immediacy with the 2019 sequel, *The Testaments*, coming out while the television series continues to be on-going. I will continue to employ the man-i-verse and the project it inspired. I am already thinking about ways I can bring in *Fight Club 3*, and I am open to suggestions because "'We miss you, Mr. Durden'...'Everything's going according to the plan'... 'We look forward to getting you back'" (Palahniuk 199).

Works Cited

Bain, Ken. *Super Courses: The Future of Teaching and Learning*. Princeton UP, 2021.

Burlingame, Christopher. "Social Identity Crisis?: Patrick Bateman, Donald Trump, and the Hermeneutic Maelstrom." *The Journal of Popular Culture*, vol. 52, no. 2, 2019, pp. 330-350.

Cassidy. "Fight Club." *Bad Games Hall of Fame*, Feb. 11, 2018, https://www.badgamehalloffame.com/fight-club/.

Collado-Rodriguez, Francisco, editor. *Chuck Palahniuk: Fight Club, Invisible Monsters, Choke*. Bloomsbury, 2013.

Eodice, Michele, et al. *The Meaningful Writing Project*. Utah State UP, 2017.

Fincher, David. *Fight Club*. Fox, 1999.

Gooblar, David. *The Missing Course: Everything They Never Taught You About College Teaching*. Harvard UP, 2019.

Hassel, Holly and Joanne Baird Giordano. "Occupy Writing Studies: Rethinking College Composition for the Needs of the Teaching Majority." *College Composition and Communication*, vol. 65, no. 1, 2013, pp. 117-139.

Hume, Kathryn. *Aggressive Fictions: Reading the Contemporary American Novel*. Cornell UP 2012.

Keesey, Douglas. *Understanding Chuck Palahniuk*. U of South Carolina P, 2016.

Kleinman, Geoffrey. "Chuck Palahniuk – Author of Fight Club." *DVDTalk*, 2007, https://www.dvdtalk.com/interviews/chuck_palahniuk.html.

Lang, James. *Distracted: Why Students Can't Focus and What You Can Do About It*. Basic, 2020.

Lang, James. "Will They Remember Writing It?" *The Chronicle of Higher Education*. Nov. 5, 2017. https://www.chronicle.com/article/will-they-remember-writing-it/.

McCracken, David. *Chuck Palahniuk and the Comic Grotesque: Subversions of Ideology in the Fiction*. McFarland, 2020.

Mookerjee, Robin. *Transgressive Fiction: The New Literary Tradition*. Palgrave Macmillan, 2013.

National Council of Teachers of English. *Professional Knowledge for the Teaching of Writing* [Position Statement]. *National Council of Teachers of English*, Feb. 28, 2016, https://ncte.org/statement/teaching-writing/.

Palahniuk, Chuck. *Fight Club*. Anchor, 2005.

——. *Make Something Up: Stories You Can't Unread*. Doubleday, 2015.

——. *Stranger than Fiction: True Stories*. Anchor, 2005.

——. Cameron Stewart, Dave Stewart, Nate Piekos, and David Mack. *Fight Club 2: The Tranquility Gambit*. Dark Horse, 2016.

Sousanis, Nick. *Unflattening*. Harvard UP, 2015.

Warner, John. *The Writer's Practice: Building Confidence in Your Nonfiction Writing*. Penguin, 2019.

——. *Why They Can't Write: Killing the Five-Paragraph Essay and Other Necessities*. Johns Hopkins UP, 2018.

Warnke, Georgia. "Hermeneutics and Social Identity." *New Literary History*, vol. 45, 2014, pp. 575-94. *ProQuest*, https://search.proquest.com/docview/1654706471/abstract/D55CE98AEDCB4A4CPQ/1.

Chapter 2

Brodentity:
Teaching Masculinity through Fight Club

Jeff Ambrose

Indiana University of Pennsylvania

Abstract: ChuckPalahniuk, in the afterword to his 1996 debut novel *Fight Club*, discusses why he wrote the book. There were many "novels that presented a social model for women to be together. To sit together and tell their stories. To share their lives. But there was no novel that presented a new social model for men to share their lives. It would have to give men the structure and roles and rules of a game – or a task - but not too touchy-feely" (214). This anti-emotional, never touchy-feely concept Palahniuk brings up is what is commonly called the bro culture. That is, the mindset among men that they must care about other men but only in ways that affirm traditional stereotypes of men. Calling someone a bro is most often a joke, a nod to the silliness of the need of a brotherhood with other men. But why is this? Why have so few before questioned male identity? Two notable exceptions are Sam Keen's nonfictional *Fire in the Belly* and the poet Robert Bly's book *Iron John*. The rise of feminism, as Palahniuk himself again says, allowed women to "sit together and tell their stories" and find their similarities and differences within the female gender. This has very rarely been done with men in modern times. In fact, the opposite, terms to criticize traditional toxic male behavior have emerged. There are the terms "neckbeard" and "nice guy", among many others, all used to describe negative male types in our current cultural climate. Thus, with this chapter, I want to begin to examine why it is so hard for men, and society at large, to talk about their feelings and what it means to actually "be a man". This will be done through analyzing instances of my teaching of the novel and the discussions it raised among students. I will make connections to other contemporary works that explore male identity but largely through affirming negative male stereotypes, such as the song "I'll Make a Man Out of You" from Disney's *Mulan* and some recent commercials.

Keywords: Chuck Palahniuk, Brodentity, masculinity, commercials

***

"In the mountains of Bolivia…men beat the crap out of one another. Drunk and bloody, they pound one another with just their bare fists, chanting, 'We are men. We are men. We are men.'" (218). So concludes the afterword of Chuck Palahniuk's 1996 debut novel, *Fight Club*. Before the Bolivia example, Palahniuk discusses why he wrote the book. There were many "novels that presented a social model for women to be together. To sit together and tell their stories. To share their lives. But there was no novel that presented a new social model for men to share their lives. It would have to give men the structure and roles and rules of a game – or a task - but not too touchy-feely" (214). Palahniuk is only half-joking. His novel does make a game of traditional masculinity with men punching in order to feel, but Palahniuk also shows the negativity of such an idea by having the narrator regularly visit support group meetings so that he can cry and sleep soundly. The anti-emotional, never touchy-feely concept Palahniuk jokes about coincides with the idea of the "bro" culture. That is, the mindset that men can care about other men but only in ways that affirm traditional stereotypes of men. As Peggy Orenstein observed in her piece for *The Atlantic*, "The Miseducation of the American Boy," many boys 16-21 could "reel off the excesses of masculinity" and recognized how "toxic" perceptions of men and "bros" are. For as much as many would like to think society has evolved views of men and women, how much has really changed in how we discuss and depict masculinity?

The rise of feminism, bourgeoned by works such as Betty Friedan's 1963 book *The Feminine Mystique*, Gloria Steinem's *Ms.* Magazine, and the impact of the Civil Rights Movement during the mid-1950s through the mid-60s, allowed women to come together and exchange accounts of their lives. Women shared stories of abuse, boredom, and dissatisfaction that spurred the creation of organizations that led to societal change and revised how women's lives are viewed. When *Fight Club* emerged in the mid-1990s, male gender was rarely examined in the same way. One exception was the poet Robert Bly's 1990 book *Iron John: A Book About Men* that was widely criticized for using the same tired trope of men as wild in the phallic setting of a forest. However, John Keen's 1992 book *Fire in the Belly: On Being a Man* remains well-regarded for its deconstruction of the aggressive male trope and its model for men to be more than a stereotype.

In this chapter, my goal is to examine how Palahniuk's *Fight Club* can be used in the college classroom for its contributions in analyzing masculinity in modern American society. Through a multi-media discussion of the novel, several "manly" product advertisements, a popular song, and social movements, I posit that *Fight Club* teaches by negation. In displaying the hyper-masculine Tyler Durden as destructive and toxic, and the narrator as passive and traditionally feminine, Palahniuk shows that a man is never one role or one type. The narrator's personality is literally fragmented by a materialistic society that demands unrealistic gendered ideals. In the first section, I frame the discussion of masculinity and media in the novel. In the second section, I showcase how I have taught *Fight Club* and how it can help students reimagine masculinity, femininity, and how society presents both in popular media.

"Put him in a dress and make him smile, and he'd be a woman" – Contextualizing Gender and Defining Brodentity

Man up. Be a man. Have some balls. Wear the pants in the relationship. We have all heard these reductive phrases before. They all relate to the concept that to be a man is to be someone physically and mentally tough, someone who keeps their feelings to themselves, and someone who is willing and able to exert physical violence to maintain their perceived status. Part of the problem is that the terms have become unconscious, thrown out or employed without realizing the implied biases and reductive nature of the words and phrases.

All of that, of course, is the problem. From those outside, often among those who have not read the book or seen the film, Palahniuk's *Fight Club* is thought to affirm this cultural degeneracy – that hyper-violent, competitive, sports-centric, sex-crazed men are the heroes. However, there is very little actual fighting in *Fight Club*, and the true villain in the book is traditional masculinity. It is personified in the character Tyler Durden, an alpha male, who is revealed to be the alternate personality of the narrator. Tyler is outgoing, a leader, sexually active, and powerful. The narrator is none of those things, and prefers decorating his apartment to going out for a beer. The narrator, once he discovers Tyler and he are the same person, realizes that Tyler is what he thought he wanted for himself. He discovers, though, that Tyler is not someone he wants to be.

Palahniuk highlights that the narrator is struggling to find happiness and identity in a materialistic modern world. He cannot cry. He cannot sleep. And he has no time or interest in developing a heterosexual love relationship. As Stephen N. Gold wrote, Palahniuk "depict[s] how ubiquitous features of modern society–advanced technology, rampant consumerism, and rapid mobility–induce, to a greater or lesser extent, a pervasive form of dissociation in its members" (14). The narrator's job is to assess car accidents and determine whether the cost of a recall outweighs the cost of lawsuits in the inevitable wrongful death suits. Essentially, he is forced every day to see people as objects, as variables in an equation. He seems to have no problem with this, though, nor does the narrator have any friends or family. Instead, he spends his time decorating his apartment with eclectic items that he truly does not care for, as he remarks that his dishes "were crafted by the honest, simple, hard-working indigenous aboriginal peoples of wherever" (Palahniuk 41). He is a socially and emotionally isolated modern man. Through these scenes, Palahniuk suggests modern men feel adrift in a sea of people as objects and objects as meaningless. In the novel, Palahniuk exhibits the need men feel, to force everything to fit into the well-defined boxes of stereotypical gender roles, instead of choosing for themselves who they are and what they want. I began teaching the novel as an exploration of toxic masculinity and the dangers of consumer culture. I believe discussions with students about stereotypes of gender and mental health are immensely rich and can aid students long after they take the course. Terry Lee, writing on violence in the film adaptation, acknowledged the artificial standards of men: "The masculinity that men enact has been developed and packaged by our culture, which insists that men perform it. Men have been conditioned to think that certain behavior is naturally masculine or not, and therefore abhorrent. They do their best to measure up" (418). The fight club itself is born out of an assumed lack of masculinity in the narrator's psyche, so Tyler fills that void for the narrator.

I set out in my literature courses to help my students think critically of the novel and what they think of society's portrayals of masculinity and femininity. Students are enmeshed in social media, many telling me they compulsively check Facebook, Twitter, and Instagram feeds. Thus, I now open my *Fight Club* unit with an article entitled "Split/Image" by the ESPN writer Kate Fagan. The article, which went on to become a best-selling book, examines Madison Holleran, a UPenn student athlete who took her own life in January of 2014. Fagan argues that Holleran's suicide was, at least in part, a result of social media standards, different and destructive for both genders, that are impossible to live in reality. Discussing this article elicits powerful responses from my students. One male student delivered an attack of the harm that filters and poses have done to self-esteem and individuality and what he observed in his high school in the changes in friends because of trends on social media.

To help frame and condense my students' and my own examination of gender, I coined the term brodentity. Brodentity is a tongue-in-cheek term, intentionally, to serve two purposes in the discussion of male identity. First, brodentity calls into question the bro culture: the hyper-masculine, stereotype-affirming thoughts and behaviors we have all heard again and again – violent, tough, powerful, bread-winner. And second, brodentity is an examination of these toxic stereotypes and how men have often been defined by what they think women are not. This opposite-driven, constantly competitive identity is the root cause of what is now called male fragility – the sensitivity and anger if not violence expressed by men when their gendered biases are pointed out to them. Jennifer Wright, writing for *Harper's Bazaar*, offered a piercing look at such angry reactions by men in her 2019 article, "The Decade of Enduring Male Fragility." My goal, then, with this term and theory, is to chart a new course for the discussion and examination of men in society and why humans feel the need to so rigidly draw a line in the sand between genders.

I recognize the concepts I associate with brodentity build on many existing ideas. In fact, we are currently flooded with terms related to brodentity – machismo, toxic masculinity, fragile masculinity, the crisis of masculinity. However, my theory is a synthesis of some of those terms and a new way of thinking about others, so I would like to unpack the key terms that paved the way for brodentity. In my courses, students and I spend about an hour going through the terms in a PowerPoint form. Once all terms have been defined, we discuss overlaps between them and gaps that may exist.

Hyper-masculinity was first studied and defined by Donald L. Mosher and Mark Sirkin in the *Journal of Research in Personality* in 1984. They associated three variables with what they call this "macho personality" – a callous sexual attitude toward women, the belief that violence is manly, and the experience of danger as exciting. Though often misunderstood to be the female counterpart to hyper-masculinity, feminism sought to have equal rights and respect afforded to both genders. This idea crystallized in the second wave of feminism in the 1960s and 70s with figures such as Kate Millett. Millett, in her bestselling 1970 book, *Sexual Politics*, argues that the personal is political and that all power-structured relationships need to be re-examined through the lens of gender to expose their biases. However, many still associate feminism with the incorrect notion that women want to have power over men or that women see men as inferior. Ironically, this is likely because the opposite had been the norm for centuries – that men have restricted women's access to education, certain jobs, and any say in government. Thus, some men see feminism as an attempt to completely tip the gendered scales in the other direction rather than as a move to balance them out. Wright spends most of her article on male fragility addressing how this idea played out in what is now referred to as #Gamergate (or Gamergate), when men attacked, harassed, and threatened women for perceived sleights as women spoke up about the mistreatment of female game creators and the over-sexualization of female characters in games. A discussion of Gamergate in my classes allows room for students to share their own opinions on men and women's equity in video games, and this slight diversion in topics still offers students ways to think critically about and engage with topics related to gender that will be addressed in Palahniuk's book.

Re-affirming masculinity due to the "threat" of feminism, directly ties into what is now referred to as male fragility. Lynn M. Ta, writing on male identity in *Fight Club*, argued that materialism is what has made masculinity go soft in society by making them consumers rather than hunters. Materialism is part of the problem, but as Wright discussed, a movement like Gamergate showcased that men get angry when women question established patriarchal structures. Men do not want to admit they have had unfair advantages in most ways in their lives. They do not want to admit their privileges and the changes and admissions that must come with embracing the desire for equality between the genders. In fact, Ta introduces this very idea through the lens of discussing David Savran. He claimed that, in light of the 1960s civil rights advances by marginalized groups, white men felt threatened and thus became violently defensive (266). In *Fight Club*, Palahniuk takes this to the extreme in the form of Project Mayhem which seeks to destroy credit institutions and museums to erase history. Because they cannot express their violent desires, and because they feel emasculated by a society that positions them as passive consumers, the men in the novel violently lash out at anyone who they perceive as putting them in such a position. J. Michael Clark agrees with Ta, writing that what *Fight Club* does is "insist that men have been emasculated by consumerism; that the post-war legacy of the so-called good life has shifted men from active, heroic, confrontational roles into the passive, ornamental roles usually assigned to women; and that, without a Great Depression, or Great War, or any other dragon to slay, emasculated men have become imprisoned in their job cubicles and possessed by their possessions" (65). This anger and angst at the emergence of feminism and feeling emasculated by their job or politics is what is called male fragility.

Male fragility is a clean transition into the current identity crisis among men. Erik Erickson coined the term identity crisis and said it can occur during the stage when one wrestles with identity cohesion versus one's role confusion. I argue that role confusion is exactly what is happening now with the #MeToo movement and the way it has put feminism front and center in many societal discussions. Because of women speaking out against male predators, men are forced to confront thoughts and behaviors which have often been normalized as "locker room talk" or "guys being guys" behaviors. I recall a student sharing their own experience with examples of hearing guys talk candidly, when believed unobserved, about the outfits and bodies of a history teacher at their school. These behaviors, which had long been ignored or laughed off, are now causes of shame and anger, and this leads to problems within those men as they either get defensive or depressed.

Competition culture is another symptom of this crisis. Men are often seen as the hunters, the sports-lovers, work over-achievers, the video game players, all activities that are rooted in competition. This competition obsession among men causes them to tie their emotional state to winning or losing a game, which should be recognized as an ultimately trivial event. This leads to many negative outcomes, the most dangerous of which is to make other things into competitions, such as arguments in a relationship wherein one must get in the last word or talk louder, or say the most hurtful thing to one-up the other. In the next section of the chapter, I discuss an example of how I teach a discussion on this very topic.

However, the final related term that informed brodentity comes from the novel itself: near-life experience. In the book, a member of Project Mayhem is driving in the oncoming traffic with Tyler/ the narrator in the car. Tyler does not care what the outcome of any accident would be. When they are run off the road and everyone in the car nearly dies, the mechanic who was driving says they just had a "near-life experience" (148). I posit this feeling of dead-while-alive or being not truly seen is one of the psychological issues plaguing men today. As a result of these negative thoughts, depression and suicide have exploded in recent decades, particularly among young men. Many do not feel they are truly alive, and they feel invisible to those around them. They feel insignificant. Thus, some seek out thrills – drugs, drinking, one-night stands, being an anonymous asshole online, and other reckless behaviors – and these rushes give them the so-called "near-life experiences." It is only when big stakes are risked that they feel something at all. In the novel, fight club and Project Mayhem are the men's way of feeling.

So where does brodentity fit in? Brodentity asks students to examine the role of feminism in creating an identity crisis in men. Doing so leads to confronting men's competition-based culture and the hyper-masculinity that is often involved. Male fragility results from questioning what has long-been seen as normal. Thus, brodentity is an umbrella term to build on these ongoing critical conversations to try to discern the potential next steps to take. How can society eliminate the toxic hyper-masculinity and competition cultures? What role exactly has feminism played in the current male identity crisis? I believe those queries are at the heart of where brodentity, as a theory, should go in its practical uses.

The famous first two rules of fight club in the novel are that you do not talk about fight club. But that is exactly the problem. So many gendered clothes and advertisements especially still rely on traditional roles and stereotypes. There are girls' sweatpants with writing across the butt or Victoria's Secret commercials with elaborate underwear. Or on the flipside, there are testosterone pill commercials about "being the real man you always knew you were" or Sport Clips' slogan of "Where it's good to be a guy" (which I will unpack later). While teaching *Fight Club*, Palahniuk screams that we need to start talking about fight club and commercials and other gendered media and what they are saying about gender and identity, and that those uncomfortable but important conversations must occur often and find their way out of the classroom.

"Tyler asked what I was really fighting" – Teaching Toxic Masculinity

I taught English for eight years at Delaware County Community College in Pennsylvania. My favorite way of engaging students was incorporating a myriad of *YouTube* videos that showed connections with the themes of the literature we covered. With *Fight Club*, I always turned first to commercials.

Many students would contest the notion that men do not talk about their feelings much or that no one really thinks men are believed to be strong, sexual beings. Tell that to advertisers, I said. I like to use SportClips and Nugenix commercials because they are so over-the-top offensive that they were the clear choice. SportClips is a haircut chain that, for years, has used the slogan, "Where it's good to be a guy." The "Big Burger Challenge" commercial depicts a few guys at a table in a sports bar. The male narrator announces "Guys live their lives a little differently" and that "We know happiness is a big screen TV." In my classes, we discuss this in the context of the *Fight Club* narrator's IKEA catalog, and there is always a spirited discussion of what makes life different for men and women. It is fascinating to have female students identify male-stereotyped possessions like video game consoles and sports cars while male students often note female-stereotyped possessions are beauty products and clothing. My classes then examine the psychology behind these possessions – what do they offer us? Are they extensions of how we feel about ourselves, or how we want others to see us? For example, students get spirited when discussing sports cars as a lame attempt to express machismo or woo women. SportClips represents a male stereotype in its "Undefeated" ad when the phrase "Hair is a game of inches" splashes across the screen. In case the viewer does not recognize the sexual connotations of men having their hair cut exclusively by young, female models in the commercials, male body image and obsession with muscle or penis size leads to class discussions of the men the narrator meets in the novel's various support groups. As Iocco wrote,

> Bob, once a champion body builder (with a chest expansion program on late-night TV) developed enormous breasts (or 'bitch tits', as Jack describes them) after having his cancerous testicles removed. We learn that Bob's status, as a physically, economically and socially castrated

man with breasts, is a product of his failed pursuit of a popular modern masculine ideal. Bob tries desperately to reassert his 'lost' masculinity through attending Remaining Men Together (a support group for men with testicular cancer) and by joining Fight Club. (50)

Bob not only loses his testicles from taking so many supplements, but he gains breasts. The name of the testicular cancer group is the apt Remaining Men Together, as if a man's biological ability to father children is his defining feature. What these ads allow in my classes is a way to bridge the fiction of the novel with ads that run every day on ESPN or the Travel Channel. Students often remark how they do not deeply "read" commercials until we analyze them critically in the context of literature. Yet, once they do, they can think of and bring to class many other examples from print and television advertisements. The added layer of irony here is the materialism aspect – Palahniuk is critiquing materialistic culture, and even 25 years later, gender stereotypes pollute many major ad campaigns, affirming the need to be critical of standardized portrayals of masculinity and femininity. For SportClips, men are shown to be sex-hungry and sport-obsessed, but that also means women are shown to be willing seductresses in the same ads. Neither men nor women are depicted realistically. The narrator in the novel has a comment that echoes both the sports and sex male ideals: "After you've been to fight club, watching football on television is watching pornography when you could be having great sex" (50). Hitting another man and being hit becomes a high better than sex. With this, Palahniuk parodies the two most common male stereotypes, being sex-and sport-crazed.

Nugenix is a "men's vitality" testosterone supplement that often uses retired athletes in their commercials. Bob from *Fight Club* is again a fitting connection. He was a champion bodybuilder but is ruined by the side effects of the supplements that temporarily helped him. In one Nugenix commercial in an airport, a married woman immediately forgets she is married when she sees Frank Thomas, a retired baseball player, who is already flanked by two women who are fawning over him. The woman asks Thomas for the secret of his physique, and after learning it is Nugenix she remarks "I wish my husband used it." *Yikes!* Further, the advertisers in each ad tout Nugenix as a "man-boosting formula" which is apparently about – you guessed it – sports and sex performance. The most confounding part of several Nugenix ads is the "clinically researched key ingredient" that they do not name, and we are just to take their word for it. In my classes, students use these ads to discuss the masculine mystique, as an homage to Friedan's satirical title *The Feminine Mystique*. Students offer their thoughts on male stereotypes from stories they know and discuss the role of those qualities in the context of the examples. These examples have ranged from "the bros at the club" who are creepy, to the bosses or co-workers who, in one my favorite phrases I have ever heard a student say, "live powerfully only on their mental islands" because they are actually insecure. Does it matter that the man is strong? Does it matter that the man sleeps around? Do these qualities represent everything about the man? In attempting to answer these questions, I have students then turn to Tyler and the narrator in *Fight Club* and consider his split personalities. What I have found is that students enjoy the relational nature of our discussions. Comparing Bob from the novel to figures they have heard of, or thinking of real-life counterparts to the narrator and Tyler allows them to think about the themes in a way that make them tangible. More than words on a page, putting real names and faces or ads and videos to the characters and ideas make the themes memorable and resonant.

The most popular-with-students comparison video I use is a sketch from the show *Key & Peele*. "I Said Bitch," features two husbands discussing their frustrations with their wives and how they assert they are the "man of the house" by calling their wife a "bitch" to their face. The humor of the sketch is that it is made clear in how they conceal this discussion and check if their wives can possibly hear, that neither of them would ever actually call their wife a bitch. The sketch parodies the "man of the house" idea that men have to be in control or the dominant personality in a relationship—that old "wear the pants in the relationship" mantra. My students have always responded to *Key & Peele* because the situations the two husbands discuss are so relatable—waiting for their wife to be ready, choosing where to go for dinner, or what movie to rent. What makes the sketch so appealing is the absurdity of the husbands' paranoia that they may be found out. They move their conversation first to the basement, then hiding in a tree in the backyard, then to an open field, and finally in a spaceship. These over-the-top locales parody the stubbornness of men and women in being right all the time, or feeling they "won" an argument. Rather than communicate openly with their partner, or compromise on an issue, the husbands will go anywhere to lie in order to appear "manly." I parallel our analysis of the sketch with the progression of fight club to Project Mayhem. Why do the men go to such lengths to feel like they are in control? This is when I teach about the second wave of feminism in the 1960s and 1970s and how *Fight Club*, and then, 15 years later, Gamergate, are, in large part, the male response to feeling threatened by women balancing out the scales of power in the workplace and the home.

A work that was released just two years after *Fight Club*, the novel, *Mulan*, the 1998 Disney animated film, shows many of the same gender stereotypes as Palahniuk's novel. The story is an adaptation of the Chinese legend Hua Mulan, a female warrior who took her father's place in the emperor's army. She concealed her gender, using the guise of being her father's son, but Mulan proved herself a great warrior and helped win the war for her kingdom. In the musical Disney adaptation, the general of the army performs a song entitled, "I'll Make a Man Out of You." The lyrics offer all the hallmarks of masculine ideal stereotypes, "You must be swift as a coursing river,/ With all the force of a great typhoon,/ With all the strength of a raging fire,/ Mysterious as the dark side of the moon." The irony of the song, and the plot of the story, is that a woman outperforms many of the men in training and in battle. Marla is the only prominent female character in Palahniuk's novel, but she is independent and more level-headed than the narrator. Thus, I use this song with my students to analyze the character of Marla and what female stereotypes she embodies or subverts like Mulan.

Parenting, or the lack of a strong male figure, specifically for the narrator, is another key aspect that my classes analyze. The narrator's father abandoned the family. At the inaugural meeting of fight club, the narrator recalls the impact of his father's leaving. "I knew my dad for about six years, but I don't remember a thing" (50). Looking out at the other men, feeling just as lost and angry as him, the narrator reflects, "What you see at fight club is a generation of men raised by women" (50). The men who attend fight club, in the narrator's mind, are as soft as he is – raised by a woman with no strong male presence in their lives. In the film adaptation, the narrator tells Tyler that, out of anyone in history, he would most want to fight is his father. Because of the lack of a father figure, the narrator feels "I'm a thirty-year-old boy, and I'm wondering if another woman is really the answer I need" (51). He has never had a man to admire or to learn from, and because he has been a man surrounded by women, the narrator does not believe a romantic relationship with a woman would be fulfilling. *But why?* I ask my students. Some reply that for the narrator every woman is haunted by the memories of his mother because she was all he had. My favorite reply was from a student who rarely spoke otherwise. The student said that the narrator has already had women in his life; he is now looking for something he has lacked. Thus, they argued, Tyler is the father/ brother he never had. Tyler is the hyper-masculine man to offset what the narrator had with his mother. As the narrator relays, "my father dumped me" (134). This phrase leads to another compelling class discussion – why the language of a break up?

Earlier, I argued that the true enemy in the novel is not Tyler, not capitalism, not materialism, but traditional masculinity threatened by the advancement of feminism and its role in forcing men to finally confront what it means to be a "man." One night, during a fight club session, the narrator nearly kills a "young guy with an angel's face" because "I was in the mood to destroy something beautiful" (Palahniuk 122). The next morning, "Tyler asked what I was really fighting," and the narrator answers, "I wanted to destroy everything beautiful I'd never have" (Palahniuk 123). This smacks of capitalism and materialism, but why does he hate beauty in the face of the man in fight club and everywhere else? Iocco contends,

> Rather than the heroic ego ideal of conventional Hollywood masculinity, Tyler is a transgressive and unpredictable spectacle of masculine excess. He is the tough muscular leader of Fight Club and Project Mayhem, but he also wears fluffy slippers and a pink towelling dressing gown with large embroidered coloured teacups. He is the embodiment of Jack's complex sense of self, which includes both masculine heterosexual virility and just a bit of camp drag. (54)

For Iocco, the narrator hates beauty in people and in objects because he feels that is what he lacks. The narrator hates what he cannot possess. Does this come from not having a father? Because of a materialistic cultural mindset? When discussing with my classes, I argue for the narrator's anger and frustration being born of perceived deficits that have been exposed by feminism. When women began to receive rights, jobs, and roles that previously only belonged to men, men reacted violently and irrationally, as Ta, Savran, and Clark acknowledged in their analyses of masculinity. This is of course not to say that feminism did anything wrong, but to open up discussions in my classes of why exactly men were so mad.

"Our culture has made us all the same" - Takeaways and Next Steps

In chapter 17 of the novel, a "space monkey," what the narrator calls the blind followers of Project Mayhem, reads out Tyler's words, "Our culture has made us all the same. No one is truly white or black or rich, anymore. We all want the same. Individually, we are nothing" (134). Men in *Fight Club* feel threatened because their unquestioned position of power has finally been questioned by a society where women and material goods have displaced some traditional male roles. The irony here is that, in fight club or Project Mayhem, the members even lose their names. They become, as the narrator always says, space monkeys – expendable parts of a faceless collective. They create what they hate. Even the systems they are fighting against, corporations and museums, were founded and are upheld primarily by white men. It takes the narrator's near-suicide to release him of his delusions and recognize the dangers he had created.

Why does teaching masculinity through *Fight Club* matter? What does it teach us? Empowering ourselves can sometimes come from empowering others such as Marla, the recruits in fight club, and the "space monkeys" given purpose in Project Mayhem. Outside of the novel, and through using companion videos and discussions, students see the wisdom in not feeling the need to constantly feel powerful. Students can begin to see the potential success in failures. We do not need to see qualities of men or women as winning for one side and losing for the other, and instead, we can imagine a society where any way of living is acceptable and enjoyable. We do not have to hide our feelings. We do not have to hold things back. We do not have to do the things the way everyone else does. Brodentity is a way to critique and examine how students think about and talk about male identity and gender at large. It allows a way to see things with a critical lens that may otherwise be left unchecked. By challenging these norms and expectations, students can expand the definitions of men and women to not be exclusionary. And, most importantly, we can do so not at the cost of one or the other, but for the benefit of all.

As Gold wrote in his article analyzing *Fight Club* as a demonstration of a society that dissociates,

> The tension between the image of power and success promoted by contemporary culture as the masculine ideal, and the reality that most men have little or no hope of attaining this coveted status is presented as yet another factor that contributes to dissociative forms of identity and experience...Intense pressure to live up to this ideal, in conjunction with the painful awareness of how distant from being able to actually attain it they are, promotes a poignantly fragmented and confused sense of self in many men. (18)

Using *Fight Club* in the college classroom to discuss masculinity, dare I say brodentity, is a powerful teaching experience. Rich conversations unfold about masculinity, media, materialism, feminism, stereotypes, and fragmented identity. The power of images to control, manipulate, and inform can be the entire basis of teaching the novel. Just as easily, perceptions of gender could be the reason the novel is included on a syllabus. Palahniuk's *Fight Club*, 25 years old as of writing (2021), proves to be a prescient and lasting critique of stereotypes and an obsession with possessing an ideal role, job, or collection of furniture.

Works Cited

Clark, J. Michael. "Faludi, *Fight Club*, and Phallic Masculinity: Exploring the Emasculating Economics of Patriarchy." *The Journal of Men's Studies*, vol. 11, no. 1, Fall 2002, pp. 65-76.

Comedy Central. "I Said Bitch." Performances by Jordan Peele and Keegan Michael-Key. *Youtube*, Feb. 1, 2012. https://www.youtube.com/watch?v=5LGEiIL1__s&t.

Fagan, Kate. "Split/Image." *ESPN*, May 7, 2015. http://www.espn.com/espn/feature/story/_/id/12833146/instagram-account-university-pennsylvania-runner-showed-only-part-story.

Gold, Steven N. "Fight Club: A Depiction of Contemporary Society as Dissociogenic." *Journal of Trauma and Dissociation*, vol. 5, no. 2, 2004, pp. 13-34.

Iocco, Melissa. "Addicted to Affliction: Masculinity and Perversity in Crash and Fight Club." *Gothic Studies*, vol. 9, no. 1, May 2007, pp. 46–56. *EBSCOhost*, https://doi.org/10.7227/GS.9.1.6.

Lee, Terry. "*Virtual Violence* in *Fight Club*: This is What Transformation of Masculine Ego *Feels* Like." *Journal of American and Comparative Cultures*, vol. 25, no. 3-4, 2002. pp. 418-423.

Mosher, Donald L. and Mark Sirkin. "Measuring a macho personality constellation." *Journal of Research in Personality*, vol. 18, no. 2, June 1984, pp. 150-163. *EBSCOhost*, https://doi.org/10.1016/0092-6566(84)90026-6.

Orenstein, Peggy. "The Miseducation of the American Boy." *The Atlantic*, January/ February 2020. https://www.theatlantic.com/magazine/archive/2020/01/the-miseducation-of-the-american-boy/603046/.

Osmond, Donny. "I'll Make a Man Out of You." *Mulan: The Motion Picture Soundtrack*, lyrics by David Sippel, Walt Disney Records, 1998, track 3.

Palahniuk, Chuck. *Fight Club*. Norton. 1996.

Script to Screen. "Nugenix Total T Airport." *YouTube*, July 29, 2019. https://www.youtube.com/watch?v=CtCV2C1jIM0.

SportClipsOfficial. "Sport Clips - Big Burger Challenge." *YouTube*, Feb. 12, 2020. https://www.youtube.com/watch?v=8aV3Jp27Fe8.

SportClipsOfficial. "Sport Clips Haircuts – Undefeated." *YouTube*, Jan. 13, 2020. https://www.youtube.com/watch?v=7MDLextU7lQ.

Ta, Lynn M. "Hurt So Good: *Fight Club*, Masculine Violence, and the Crisis of Capitalism." *The Journal of American Culture*, vol. 29, no. 3, September 2006, pp. 265-277. *EBSCOhost*, https://doi.org/10.1111/j.1542-734X.2006.00370.x.

Wright, Jennifer. "The Decade of Enduring Male Fragility." *Harper's Bazaar*, Dec. 27, 2019. https://www.harpersbazaar.com/culture/features/a30324982/rise-of-online-harassment-decade-of-male-fragility/.

Chapter 3

Teaching Creative Writing, Literary Theory, and Critical Race Theory with Palahniuk

Nicole Lowman

State University of New York

Abstract: Within the first few chapters of *Fight Club*, we encounter a hypothetical dildo in the narrator's suitcase and another on Marla Singer's dresser. In my writing about literature courses, we discuss the Foucauldian regulation at play and the pleasure the airline agent gets from lecturing passengers with vibrating luggage. The latter is "made of the same soft pink plastic as a million Barbie dolls" and Tyler imagines the two products "coming off the same assembly line in Taiwan." These scenes alongside one another foster a fruitful discussion about American outsourcing of cheap labor and mass production, as well as conceptions of white male masculinity and sexual potency. In my creative writing class, *Fight Club* helps my students understand the narrative point of view, pacing, and description. Palahniuk's unique figures of speech give us a model for moving beyond the cliche. Students are aware of figurative language but often reproduce well-worn phrasing like "hard as a rock," which are visibly dull when compared with Palahniuk's "broken noses spreading out like an eggplant" and "his ass is a loaf of white bread." In both courses, we discuss how frequent vacillations between first and second-person narration create unease and urgency. I help my creative writing students understand how the narrator's psychological instability is revealed through the way his narration rapidly alternates between thoughts about fight club, Tyler's father, and his own father. His insecurity about his own masculinity and his discontent with consumer capitalism is "shown" (rather than "told") when the narrator thinks that because of fight club, "he could get [his] hands on everything in the world that didn't work, ...the bank that says [he's] hundreds of dollars overdrawn." While these courses have different focuses, the material is mutually resonant, and my work in one informs my teaching in the other and has led to considering ways to build off this foundation by exploring Critical Race Theory with *Adjustment Day*.

Keywords: Fight Club, Adjustment Day, Critical Race Theory, Creative Writing, Literary Studies

***

> [W]ith our culture so equally divided, the only way to introduce new possibilities or insights will be by making them entertaining. If the audience feels served and entertained, they're more likely to tolerate a different viewpoint. No one wants to spend their time and money getting preached at so any kind of a message must first be entertaining.
> —Chuck Palahniuk, as quoted in *Sacred and Immoral: On the Writings of Chuck Palahniuk* (Sartain 181)

The above is the beginning of Chuck Palahniuk's response to what prompted him to experiment with genre fiction in *Haunted*, particularly in a time of political tensions. The interview with Matt Kavanagh took place in early 2005, so the tensions have only tightened, but the message remains the same, and, as much as we probably want to avoid it, the message applies to teaching at the college level, especially in introductory and required courses, largely taken by non-majors. These are the classes I've taught in western New York, and they are the classes that most college and university instructors teach in an increasingly adjunctified higher education landscape. Students in this consumer capitalist mayhem we call 21st century America sometimes think that professors and college instructors work for them. I recall explaining to different students in different courses in different semesters at different institutions that they do not, in fact, pay my salary. If they did, I wouldn't be paid less than they pay for the class I'm teaching, especially since there are at least 17, sometimes 23, other students. At some institutions, adjunct pay is less than a single student pays for a 3-credit course. My point is not that we should simply bow to students' whims or succumb to this inaccurate and toxic consumer mindset by constantly trying to please and amuse our students, but that maybe Palahniuk has a point. If we want to introduce new ideas, ways of thinking, and ways of doing, we might do well to provide some points of entertainment. Such entertainment can foster critical thinking while providing a vehicle for achieving other curricular goals.

Palahniuk's work is not only entertaining but also rife with literary devices, references to history, and complex character development, so it can be a great tool for instructors in a number of English and Cultural Studies courses.

What's great about Palahniuk's work is it piques students' interest while demonstrating a number of literary techniques and elements and illustrates literary and cultural theory through its scenes, themes, and characters. As one of my students wrote in their creative writing journal, "*Fight Club* has never not captivated me," and I argue that instructors can begin from this point of captivation to reach curricular goals.

Though a number of Palahniuk's novels and short stories provide similar opportunities for instructors, this chapter focuses on *Fight Club*, which I have successfully taught in first-year writing and creative writing courses. In my creative writing classes, *Fight Club* helps my students understand the narrative point of view, pacing, and description. Palahniuk's unique figures of speech give us a model for moving beyond the cliche. Students are aware of figurative language but often reproduce well-worn phrasing like "hard as a rock," which Palahniuk refers to as "received text" in his discussion of minimalist writing ("Not Chasing Amy"). He recommends instead including "something funny or profound enough you'll remember it for years" and "describ[ing] actions and appearances in a way that makes a judgment occur in the reader's mind. Whatever it is, you unpack it into the details that will reassemble within the reader." This latter technique is called "recording angel" in minimalism, and it means that "every sentence isn't crafted, it's tortured over." Received text is visibly dull when compared with something like Palahniuk's "steam shovel jaw like a marketing tool tanned the color of a barbecued potato chip" (48). In Literary Perspectives, an advanced first-year writing course, I couple *Fight Club* with excerpts from Sigmund Freud after we've already discussed excerpts from Michel Foucault and Max Horkheimer and Theodor Adorno. In both courses, we discuss how frequent vacillations between first- and second-person narration create unease and urgency. I help my creative writing students understand how the narrator's psychological instability is revealed through the way his narration rapidly alternates between thoughts about fight club, Tyler's father, and his own father. His insecurity about his own masculinity and his discontent with consumer capitalism is "shown" (rather than "told") when the narrator thinks that because of fight club, "he could get [his] hands on everything in the world that didn't work, ...the bank that says [he's] hundreds of dollars overdrawn" (53). I haven't yet taught *Adjustment Day*, but I will also suggest opportunities for instructors interested in incorporating critical race theory into their course content to do so with this novel because it seems to expand upon work Palahniuk began more than 20 years before in *Fight Club*. This chapter is separated by pedagogical aim, so teachers of a variety of courses can easily navigate to the appropriate section.

Teaching Creative Writing with "Fight Club"

> So I read this out loud to my boyfriend and we both loved it. I think we both related to it (not in the sense that we want to beat people up) but because the characters were so human. And it's like, we're human. It's weird. —Student Journal, Introduction to Creative Writing, Fall 2018

Obviously, my student was being a bit playful in their journal, but the sentiment underlying their entry is the reason I assign Palahniuk's "Fight Club" in my Introduction to Creative Writing class: it's a masterclass in character development and audience engagement. The title of Palahniuk's most well-known novel is in quotation marks above because we only read chapter six of the novel. For the uninitiated, chapter six of *Fight Club* was initially published as a short story that Palahniuk then expanded into his now-iconic novel, which was then adapted to the now-iconic movie. Many students are familiar with the story, likely from the film, but even if they aren't, this chapter helps me illustrate a number of skills that are foundational to short story writing: character development, narrative point of view, fictional time, and figurative language. Seeing how successfully Palahniuk executes these techniques in fewer than eight pages also provides a model for my students as they craft an original short story of similar length to submit as their midterm. In this section, I'll review the basic structure of my creative writing course, including where Palahniuk fits in thematically and chronologically, and how Palahniuk's short story helps illustrate key elements of short story writing for my students.

I devote the first half of the semester to studying fiction, and there are ten stories on the class calendar, alongside chapters from somewhat of a textbook: *On Writing Short Stories*, edited by Tom Bailey. For each class period, we study a particular story or set of stories in the context of one of the elements from our textbook. In the first week, we talk about how to read as a writer—looking for the techniques that make us want to keep reading and thinking about how we can execute them ourselves—and the concept of plot. We continue thinking about writerly practices by watching Kurt Vonnegut's presentation on the shape of stories and reading Palahniuk's 13 writing tips, shared in various writing blogs. My goal with these first readings is to get students thinking that writing is a continuous process, that readers have expectations that writers must meet but also challenge, and that characters and how they respond to what happens around them are the driving forces of stories.

Both our textbook and the short fiction on my syllabus (and, arguably, any story worth reading) demonstrate the critical value of complex, thinking characters whose motivations drive the plot. The first story we read is

Vonnegut's "Harrison Bergeron" at the close of week one, followed by Ernest Hemingway's "Hills Like White Elephants" and Stephen King's "Premium Harmony" at the beginning of week two. We discuss what the textbook says about character and plot that's relevant here. At the end of week two, we shift to narrative point of view and discuss how "each choice of POV has its advantages and disadvantages, its freedoms and limitations" (Bailey 30). We read and analyze the differences between first-, second-, and third-person narration through three short stories with strong and unique narrative voice.

Palahniuk's "Fight Club," written mainly in first person, shows up on the syllabus at the end of week two with a section of Jamaica Kincaid's "A Small Place," written mostly in second person, and Flannery O'Connor's "Everything that Rises Must Converge," written in third person. Students are focused on a narrative point of view, so the first thing I ask in class is which narrative style the author has chosen, and we discuss the potential benefits and drawbacks of each style. The students noted that the third person in O'Connor does this but has that disadvantage. Kincaid likely choose second person to impose upon her reader the way tourists impose upon Antiguans. Students inevitably notice that "Fight Club" is in the first person but often fail to notice the second person. The fun part is discussing how the unnamed narrator's vacillation between first and second person can affect the reader's experience of the text.

Our textbook tells us that first-person narration has the benefit of a very strong voice in narration that can only be acquired through really trying to "*be*" the narrator, and that second person can both distance the narrator from the events of the text and impose those events on the reader (Bailey 30-33). At first glance, when the narrator says, "Fight club gets to be your reason for going to the gym and keeping your hair cut short and cutting your nails," readers might simply feel like the narrator is talking to them (Palahniuk, *Fight Club* 50). When students look more closely, though, we see that at least in some passages, the narrator is talking about himself but using the second person. For example, he describes a hypothetical where "maybe at lunch, the waiter comes to your table" looking busted up from fight club, and "you don't say anything because fight club only exists in the hours between when fight club starts and when fight club ends" (Palahniuk, *Fight Club* 48). Immediately after this hypothetical, the narrator describes how "you saw the kid who works in the copy center, [...] but this kid was a god for ten minutes when you saw him kick the air out of an account representative twice his size…" (Palahniuk, *Fight Club* 48-49). These are obviously both experiences that the narrator has had that he wants readers to imagine happening to themselves, so they'll be able to understand how exhilarating fight club is.

The realization that the narrator is trying to transpose his own emotions onto readers reinforces our textbook's claim that "through the eyes, perceptions or directions of the narrator or narration, we *view* (i.e., *experience*) the story" (Bailey 29, original emphasis). Students discuss how they not only experience the narrator's positive feelings about fight club but also the general unease and urgency created by his frequent vacillations between first- and second-person narration. These vacillations, along with rapid transitions between thoughts about fight club, Tyler's father, and the narrator's father, suggest the narrator's psychological instability. While the shift between topics and style of narration might evoke a kind of natural dialogue, that dialogue is necessarily one-sided and how the narrator experiences his interactions with Tyler. The short story doesn't reveal that Tyler is a psychic double, but it definitely implies it through narrative techniques like point-of-view shifts and small moments like Tyler telling hospital workers that the narrator "fell down" and the narrator saying, "Sometimes, Tyler speaks for me. I did this to myself" (Palahniuk, *Fight Club* 52). One might not know the narrator has a double from reading only this short story, but these moments and the knowledge of the extended story demonstrate how the writer needs to know more about the characters than they can show in the span of the story. "Fight Club" demonstrates that short story writers must create a whole world for their characters, know everything about that world, and decide which elements to show in the short amount of time they have.

As we focus on setting and fictional time with Shirley Jackson's "The Lottery" and Zora Neal Hurston's "How It Feels to Be Colored Me," I remind my students of how Palahniuk dealt with time and set the scene. Students read in the textbook that "fictional time can be *felt* through the dramatization of events that make up a short story...The scene puts the story into present time, allowing us to see and hear what the characters are seeing and hearing... Scene, because it gives direct experience, is the foundation of fictional time" (Bailey 61). Palahniuk opens his story *in media res*—in the middle of the action—which is often necessary in a short story, especially the length my students write. There isn't time for them to give a huge backstory, so I remind students of how they learned so much about the narrator through his thoughts and actions in the opening scene: He's in a conference room, in the middle of a presentation he created that his boss, who doesn't know the material, is giving because his boss "won't let [him] run the demo with a black eye and half my face swollen from the stitches inside my cheek" (Palahniuk, *Fight Club* 47). Right off the bat, the reader knows that the narrator works in the corporate world, is some kind of worker rather than manager, and that he has been involved in something violent that has disfigured his face. None of this is "told," however, it is all "shown."

My creative writing students often struggle with showing character attributes and plot points rather than didactically telling the details; Palahniuk's unique figures of speech give students a model for moving beyond the cliché. Students are aware of figurative language but often reproduce well-worn phrasing like "blue as the sky" and "sweet as pie." These are a good starting point, but they pale in comparison to Palahniuk's "the two black eyes of a giant panda" and "the black stitches on a dog after it's been fixed" (48; 47). Palahniuk's descriptions demonstrate how a "story can be a succession of tasty, smelly, touchable details," which can "give the reader a sympathetic physical reaction [and] involve the reader on a gut level" ("Not Chasing Amy"). In other words, Palahniuk gives readers and students concrete examples of what it means to "show" rather than "tell" when the narrator says his dad "starts a new family in a new town about every six years. This isn't so much like a family as it's like he sets up a franchise," rather than a general, telling detail like "I had a bad relationship with my dad" (Palahniuk, *Fight Club* 50) This metaphor helps students talk about how the narrator's insecurity about his masculinity and his discontent with consumer capitalism is "shown" (rather than "told"). Instead of the narrator explicitly saying something like "I had no power in my job, so I figured I should punch random dudes to make myself feel better," he thinks to himself fight club lets him get his "hands on everything in the world that didn't work" like his "cleaning that came back with the collar buttons broken" and his bank account that is "hundreds of dollars overdrawn" (Palahniuk, *Fight Club* 53). Taking these points together highlights the need for precision in writing—as our textbook says, "to make something crystal clear, to reduce to essence"—especially in figurative language (Palahniuk, *Fight Club* 87).

As students study the published short stories of well-known writers throughout the semester, we discern criteria for a "good" short story, which becomes the rubric for their midterm short stories. The rubric discussion inevitably contains references to "Fight Club," and students always remember how engaged they were with that story. I ask what engaged them, and how we can take specifics about "Fight Club" and expand them into overarching criteria for any short fiction. Though Palahniuk's short story is compact, we end up concluding that it is a masterclass in description, unique figurative language, character development, pacing, and narrative voice. We only "officially" talk about "Fight Club" for one class period, and discuss it alongside two other short stories, but it keeps coming up throughout our fiction unit, and even into poetry when we continue to develop figures of speech to evoke emotion.

Teaching Literary Theory with Fight Club

It is a book about what it means to reach the absolute lowest point in one's life. Although I have yet to personally reach this breaking point, it intrigues me.... It blows my mind that the euphoria following this massive release of pent up energy is so strong that one could keep coming back week after week just to get the snot beaten out of them.... The message being that everyone is exactly the same in their needs; just a collection of nameless, faceless pawns of society.... Everyone is what someone else believes they are. The desire to keep beating other men and getting beaten by other men stems from the fact that they all just want to beat what they hate about themselves out of themself. – Student Journal, Literary Perspectives, Fall 2018

Palahniuk's writing can interest students in the ways that literature addresses societal issue while provoking critical thinking, and my Literary Perspectives student above illustrates as much in their journal entry. I'm not sure that I entirely agree with my student's assessment of what *Fight Club* is about, but the important point for my purposes is that because students can relate to the narrator's relationship with societal expectations, they are engaged in the text, and that engagement opens the door to understanding and applying some basics of literary theory. These skills are necessary learning outcomes of many second-semester, first-year writing courses, as well as in literature courses.

Each section of Literary Perspectives, a writing intensive course where students argue their own interpretations of texts using critical theoretical approaches, has an instructor-designed theme, and the theme of my course is "Americanness, masculinity, and religion." We focus on a selection of literary and cultural production beginning with James Baldwin's *The Fire Next Time* and concluding with Childish Gambino's "This Is America." Other primary texts include—in the order they appear on the syllabus—President John F. Kennedy's 1963 speech on racial inequality and civil rights, Kurt Vonnegut's *Breakfast of Champions*, Toni Morrison's *Beloved*, Palahniuk's *Fight Club*, David Fincher's film version of the novel, Ta-Nehisi Coates' *The Beautiful Struggle*, and Kendrick Lamar's "HUMBLE." With each primary text, we read excerpts of relevant critical theory from the second edition of Julie Rivkin and Michael Ryan's *Literary Theory: An Anthology* to help us consider the question underlying the course: How does each artist or author critique "Americanness, masculinity, and religion" even as they incorporate those ideas into their texts? By the time we begin discussing *Fight Club*, we have had a primer on Max Horkheimer and Theodor Adorno's concept of the culture industry and Michel Foucault's *The History of Sexuality*, and these theories supplement our foray into psychoanalysis with Palahniuk. With *Fight Club*, we study the fundamentals of Freudian psychoanalysis, specifically as they relate to the uncanny. For the remainder of this section, I'll review the theories *Fight Club* allows me to illustrate for my students and suggest portions of the text that have worked well in my courses.

Within the first few chapters of *Fight Club*, we encounter two dildos, which many students find somewhat hilarious and also provide a springboard for discussing Foucauldian regulation and consumer capitalism. In *Sacred and Immoral: On the Writings of Chuck Palahniuk*, Ron Riekki writes that "Foucault's specific examination on the intersection of individual subjectivity and social discipline makes him an especially valuable theorist for investigations of Palahniuk's fiction" (98). Riekki links Foucault's concept of regulation by "carceral 'apparatuses'" and Louis Althusser's ideological state apparatuses (ISAs) (89), which constitute a valuable avenue for discovering foundational literary theory, but misses what seems an obvious foray into Foucault via Palahniuk, especially in *Fight Club*: sexuality and what Foucault calls "the perverse implantation" (892). Of course, in Foucault's analysis, sexuality and perversity are regulated through what Althusser would call ISAs, but considering sexuality on its own terms seems important in a homoerotic text like *Fight Club* that includes, among other things, images of penises spliced into movie reels and dildos.

The first dildo in *Fight Club* is only hypothetical and potentially in the narrator's suitcase. He is stopped by security at Dulles airport because the electric razor in his luggage vibrated, which could mean a bomb. According to "the security task force guy," once in a while, the sound and movement is "a vibrating dildo," and he goes on to describe the embarrassment that ensues when confronting the passenger:

> Imagine, the task force guy says, telling a passenger on arrival that a dildo kept her baggage on the East Coast. Sometimes it's even a man. It's airline policy not to imply ownership in the event of a dildo. Use the indefinite article.
>
> A dildo.
>
> Never your dildo.
>
> Never, ever say the dildo accidentally turned itself on.
>
> A dildo activated itself and created an emergency situation that required evacuating your baggage. (Palahniuk, *Fight Club* 42)

Students chuckle at this scene, particularly because I read it out loud, and I ask what is funny about the situation. The general consensus is that they aren't used to hearing an instructor talk about dildos, and that someone finding someone else's dildo in public is embarrassing, especially if it's a man's dildo.

These responses help me to illustrate Foucault's claim that there is both power and pleasure in repression, that the repression itself is a form of power that induces pleasure. Foucault describes how this interaction between power and pleasure "produced a twofold effect: an impetus was given to power through its very exercise; an emotion rewarded the overseeing control and carried it further; the intensity of the confession renewed the questioner's curiosity; the pleasure discovered fed back to the power that encircled it" (896-97). In Palahniuk's fictional scenario, the security agent acts as the questioner who clearly feels a sense of pleasure in the power he has to, in effect, reveal the passengers' perversity. A female with a dildo is perverse enough, but a man with a dildo seems the height of perversion, so much so that the security agent can't even pursue that train of thought. The airline's policy not to imply ownership suggests that the airline does not want to force a false confession, thereby accusing the passenger of perversity. However, holding and inspecting the vibrating bag acts as a kind of Foucauldian "questioning" about the bag's contents and the owner's activities with its contents. The security agent's heightened curiosity about the unattributed dildo owner's sexual proclivities creates its own kind of pleasure. According to Foucault, that is reinforced by the power the agent has to imply the passenger's perversity, even as the implication is supposedly nullified by using the indefinite article. The dildo itself is relegated to perversity because it calls to mind sexual expression that does not lead to the reproduction of the labor force, demonstrating the way that the regulation of sexuality is connected to the perpetuation of capitalism (Foucault 892).

The interconnection between compulsory heterosexual reproduction and the reproduction of capitalism is further demonstrated just a few pages later by the dildo on Marla's dresser. Palahniuk writes that the dildo is "made of the same soft pink plastic as a million Barbie dolls" and Tyler imagines the two products "coming off the same assembly line in Taiwan" (Palahniuk, *FC* 61). The description of the dildo and Tyler's thoughts about it only comprise a paragraph, but that paragraph provides another concrete example of Horkheimer and Adorno's theories on the culture industry. Horkheimer and Adorno argue that companies create ostensibly different products using the same materials, and these supposed differentiations play a role in "classifying, organizing, and labeling consumers" (1243). Horkheimer and Adorno outline a hierarchy of cars, for example, that Lexus is considered a "luxury" version of Toyota, and discuss how the brand of car signifies social class and economic standing, despite both products being made from the same material and in the same factory. They argue that even though these cars are said to be "mechanically differentiated," they "prove to be all alike in the end" (Horkheimer and Adorno1243). At first, this seems like a stretch to my students. How are cars related to dildos and Barbie dolls, they wonder. Like the Toyota and the Lexus, the dildo and Barbie are made from the same materials, and, like the two-car brands, the two pink plastic items signify a different position in the cultural hierarchy. The Barbie illustrates the respectable use of the pink plastic since the dolls are made for young children, the result of state-sanctioned heterosexual reproduction. The dildo, on the other hand, is an illustration of a perverse, culturally "lower" use of the pink plastic. That both items are pink highlights the cultural femininity of the two products, recalling the gendered regulation of sexual perversion mentioned above.

Marla's response to this brief dildo scene helps me transition to some foundational concepts of Freudian psychoanalysis, which is the main theoretical focus of the approach to *Fight Club*. Marla notices the narrator or Tyler looking at the dildo and tells him not to worry, that the dildo isn't a threat to him. The premise of Marla's comment, of course, is the cultural conception that masculinity is tied to heterosexual potency and that if Marla kept and used the dildo, then the man she was sleeping with must not be satisfying her. This cultural conception is arguably a manifestation of what Freud would call castration anxiety. The dildo is a literal replacement for the penis, a physical manifestation of the psychic phallus. One of the psychoanalytic texts my students read is Freud's essay, "The Uncanny," which further connects the dildo, the Barbie, and castration anxiety.

Before we get to "The Uncanny," though, my students read Rivkin and Ryan's introduction to their psychoanalysis section, and I ask them to focus mainly on the concepts of repression and the Oedipus complex, the theories we will use most. Most readers are likely familiar with these concepts, but in brief, Freud posits that as children grow into adults, they learn to suppress unacceptable desires into their unconscious, so they can function as acceptable members of society. One such desire is that for sexual possession of the mother, which Freud argues was played out in the story of the mythical Oedipus, hence naming the complex after him. Freud insists that the complex manifests differently along gender lines, in order to ensure socially acceptable gender identification and heterosexuality. All children desire their mothers and come to identify themselves through either the presence or absence of the penis. Boys see that their mothers lack a penis, which triggers the fear that they, too, might lose theirs, and they renounce their sexual desire for their mother, so their father will not castrate them. Girls begin with no penis, and when they notice their mothers' apparent castration, they turn their hatred onto the mother for denying them the penis in the first place and their affection onto the father. All these desires are socially unacceptable because of the incest taboo, which Freud says we can trace back to Oedipus, and every child must repress these desires into the unconscious.

Once we arrive at "The Uncanny," then, my students have a general understanding of Freudian concepts, and we discuss the connections between what they read about the Oedipus complex, the uncanny, and the dildo on Marla's dresser. In the essay, Freud does a close reading of a German story called "The Sand-Man," taking as a starting point the analysis of one of his contemporaries. His contemporary argued that the uncanny was most easily seen in instances where something inanimate has lifelike qualities, making individuals question whether that object is real. In "The Sand-Man," the main character falls in love with a doll, and Freud suggests that if humans use his contemporary's theory, they would likely stop at thinking that was the uncanny bit and end at that. However, Freud argues that there is more to the story, and thus more to the uncanny, than that. The lifelike doll in "The Sand-Man" has her eyes removed by a character that elicits terror in the main character, and Freud maintains that the terror is not attached to the lifelike doll, but to the removal of her eyes, a violence that he argues is symbolic of castration. As evidence, he points to the fact that the main character remembers The Sand-Man as a figure that "tears out children's eyes" and that the mythical Oedipus tore out his own eyes as "a mitigated form of the punishment of castration" (422; 424). As such, the removal of the doll's eyes reminds the main character of his castration anxiety, which he has repressed. According to Freud, individuals experience the uncanny when the repressed returns, but because it returns in a different form, it feels familiar but also foreign. Applying this to the brief moment in Marla's room, students see that the "millions of baby dolls and Barbie dolls and dildos injection-molded and coming off the same assembly line in Taiwan" would create an uncanny feeling of castration anxiety in Tyler (who has gone to see Marla) (Palahniuk, *Fight Club* 61). Marla flippantly comments, "Don't be afraid. It's not a threat to you," but, according to Freud, that pink plastic and the commodities it has been shaped into are an acute threat to Tyler's (the narrator's) psyche.

Returning to this brief moment in Marla's room after the first-time reader of *Fight Club* realizes that Tyler is the narrator's psychic double reveals the textual hint Palahniuk provided here about the narrator's psychic instability. As glossed above, repression is necessary for Freud but "also creates what might be called a second self" which encompasses "all that cannot for one reason or another be expressed or realized in civil life" (Rivkin and Ryan 389). These unconscious processes and their results lead to "'uncanny' feelings of doubleness, or a sense that something strange coexists with what is most familiar" (Rivkin and Ryan 390). Uncanny moments such as these, where the narrator, via his psychic double, is reminded of his repressed castration anxiety further illustrate the double's connection with the return of the repressed in Freud's theory. As the novel unfolds, students further recognize the double's association with "the ghastly harbinger of death" when Tyler tells the narrator, "The last thing we have to do is your martyrdom thing. Your big death thing" (Freud 424; Palahniuk, *Fight Club* 203). Throughout the text, beginning with the opening scene where the narrator mentions "Tyler's whole murder-suicide thing," we can trace Freud's theory, as if Palahniuk read psychoanalytic theory while writing the novel (Palahniuk, *Fight Club* 13).

One telltale narrative technique that reveals the narrator is telling a story of him and his psychic double that I mentioned earlier when discussing creative writing pedagogy is his tendency to alternate between using the first and second person, sometimes in the same sentence. Early in the novel, when the narrator is explaining his compulsion to attend support groups for people with terminal illnesses, he says, "This is when I'd cry because right now, your life comes down to nothing, and not even nothing, oblivion" (Palahniuk, *Fight Club* 17). Looking at instances such as this one creates an opportunity to discuss how this style of narrative affects the reader. Is Palahniuk trying to jar his reader? Insert the reader directly into the narrator's subject position? Are these moments to question which character—the narrator or his double—is actually narrating?

These kinds of narrative questions are eliminated by watching David Fincher's film adaptation, which the class does to close out the unit on *Fight Club*. In the novel, the narrator's speech is only in quotation marks when he is functioning as Tyler, yet all other characters speak with traditional dialogue markers. Fincher's film uses voiceover for some of the narrator's internal monologue, but that textual difference is lost. My students and I discuss the value the first-person novel provides of occupying the viewpoint of the narrator as opposed to viewing a story predominantly from the protagonist's perspective but still looking at that character as a third person. In other words, the primary lens of the film is the camera, rather than the narrator himself. Students find it fun that they can watch a movie version of the text, and having a popular film and a printed novel to compare also helps my students see that there are some things words just do better, while also recognizing the difficulty of creating emotions without physical visuals, and the power words have to facilitate that visualization.

Possibilities for *Adjustment Day*: Critical Race Theory, Metafiction, and *Fight Club*

"The last thing a [B]lack man wants to be is another fake white man.... The last thing a white man wants to be is another phony paragon." — The Talbott Book (Palahniuk, *Adjustment Day* 95).

In Chuck Palahniuk's *Adjustment Day*, a new world order begins as a result of a violent overthrow by disempowered men. The main actors in the text, then, hold a strikingly similar societal position "God's middle children... with no special place in history and no special attention" that drive the action of *Fight Club* (Palahniuk, *Fight Club* 141). In *Adjustment Day*, Talbott Reynolds instructs Walter Baines to recruit men from Narcotics Anonymous, "men who'd given up on life. Younger men. Angry and disillusioned men" to become chieftains in the new world order (219). These men begin three new societies, segregated by race and sexuality and guided by the tenets espoused in The Talbott Book, quoted above. Talbott is arguably a Tyler Durden figure, only if Project Mayhem achieved its aims on a national scale. *The Guardian, NPR,* and reviewers all over *Good Reads* have noted these similarities, and Palahniuk self-consciously includes metafictional references to *Fight Club* and himself in *Adjustment Day*. These elements offer opportunities to pursue the ways the *Adjustment Day* might be considered an extension of *Fight Club*—despite the metafictional assertion that it is not—and the culturally resonant social and political conflicts suggest further possibilities for accomplishing a number of pedagogical aims from understanding queer theory to illustrating historicism (Palahniuk, *Adjustment Day* 157). While I have yet to teach *Adjustment Day*, the novel is rich with potential avenues to introduce Critical Race Theory, particularly to white students.

Critical Race Theory (CRT) developed in legal studies during the mid-to-late 1980s and gained national, mainstream attention during the 2020 presidential election cycle. CRT began as a "race-based, systematic critique of legal reasoning and legal institutions themselves" that is intended to "to reveal and challenge the practices of subordination facilitated and permitted by legal discourse and legal institutions" (Harris xv, xvi). Most Americans are taught that their society is one based on equity, and that the 1964 Civil Rights Act made theirs a colorblind society, so CRT can be said to run counter to American mythologies or what some of the theory's founders call "the assumptions about racial matters most of us absorb from the cultural heritage in which we come of age in the United States" (Delgado and Stefancic 2). As such, in September 2020, then President Donald Trump signed an executive order banning CRT from federal trainings, calling the theory "divisive anti-American propaganda" (Kelly; Street). When Joe Biden took office, he reversed

Trump's policy with one an executive order that encouraged agencies "to ensure that it is accounting for, and taking appropriate steps to combat, overlapping forms of discrimination, such as discrimination on the basis of race or disability people" (Street; Biden). These successive executive orders suggest the polarization of the American public on the topic of racial matters and how those matters play into the cultural consciousness.

Palahniuk's *Adjustment Day* ventriloquizes the contemporary polarization around race and thus provides an opportunity for addressing these issues in the classroom, especially with white male students, who often want to avoid or challenge the topic. Teacher and scholar Adam Ellwanger identifies himself as "a white, Christian, heterosexual man with conservative and libertarian political tendencies" who is looking for "ways that teachers can offer white students a practical reason to buy into discussions of race in the classroom" because, he suggests that, many approaches from critical race theory make "silence about whiteness... the safest, most attractive, most polite choice for white students" (36, 37, 38). Ultimately, Ellwanger offers a litany of critiques of CRT and a prescription for "the discursive process of reinventing whiteness," "an exploration of what whiteness might be," and "the discovery of new, affirmative, nonracist ways for whiteness to speak itself" (55). While I find his treatment of the issue mostly unhelpful, I take his perspective—similar to that of white conservative students that many CRT teachers would like to reach—and offer that Palahniuk's text not only explores racial division and an example of what "reinventing whiteness" might look like but also "offer[s] white students a practical reason buy into discussions of race."

There is not enough space here to fully engage Palahniuk's 316-page novel, but I'd like to suggest a starting point for engaging CRT through *Adjustment Day*. A central thrust of CRT is the concept that "race and races are products of social thought and relations. Not objective, inherent, or fixed, they correspond to no biological or genetic reality; rather, races are categories that society invents, manipulates, or retires when convenient" (Delgado and Stefancic 9). Similarly, the Talbott book, which spurs the three ethnostates of the new world order in *Adjustment Day*, posits that Black Americans are in underprivileged positions because of long-established social relations, and those relations are drastically altered when Black and white separate. For example, in the white ethnostate the preferred mode of address is "white speak," a debased Renaissance-style English, where men wear codpieces and kilts, demonstrating one admittedly satirical possibility of "what whiteness might be" (285). Black and white work together in order to separate, and the Talbott book that they all follow asserts that "the [B]lack thug conducts gang violence [to] demonstrate political identity," and the central Black character, Jamal, thinks later in the novel how, prior to the titular Adjustment Day, he "had always played the submissive good guy because the only other role was to be a thug" (Palahniuk *Adjustment Day* 72; 160). While the repetition of these stereotypes has the potential to reinforce them in the minds of some readers, the ehtnostates ultimately fail, suggesting that such divisions according to race are ill-advised. The division into ethnostates, and the Talbott book that spans that division, however, opens a conversation about the social thought and relations that perpetuate racial inequality and provides a vehicle for students to learn about Critical Race Theory and practice applying it in a lower-stakes environment.

Conclusion

I have proposed three different "uses" for Chuck Palahniuk in the university classroom: creative writing, literary theory, and critical race studies. I should note that I do not have years of data to support the claims made in this chapter, only the anecdotal evidence provided from teaching two sections of Literary Perspectives and two sections of Intro to Creative Writing, both to just under 40 students total. Nonetheless, the suggestions here are based on the ways that Palahniuk's *Fight Club* has provided me, and the students I taught, opportunities for engaging in the curricular goals of both courses, which can be adapted to other courses. I have not yet taught *Adjustment Day*, but if my experience teaching *Fight Club* is any indicator, Palahniuk's work can help instructors bridge difficult topics with potentially resistant students. This is not to say that college instructors should strive to placate the students, only to suggest that teachers and students can have a little fun and entertainment while reaching curricular goals.

Works Cited

"Adjustment Day." *Good Reads*. Good Reads, Inc., 2021. https://www.goodreads.com/book/show/41817499-adjustment-day.

Bailey, Tom, editor. *On Writing Short Stories*. 2nd ed. Oxford UP, 2011.

Baldwin, James. *The Fire Next Time. James Baldwin Collected Essays*. 1963. Library of Congress, 1998.

Beaumont-Thomas, Ben. "*Fight Club* Author Chuck Palahniuk on His Book Becoming a Bible for the Incel Movement." *The Guardian*. 20 July 2018. https://www.theguardian.com/books/2018/jul/20/chuck-palahniuk-interview-adjustment-day-black-ethno-state-gay-parenting-incel-movement.

Biden, Joseph R. "Executive Order on Preventing and Combating Discrimination on the Basis of Gender Identity or Sexual Orientation." *White House*, White House, 20 Jan. 2021, https://www.whitehouse.gov/briefing-room/presidential-actions/2021/01/20/executive-order-preventing-and-combating-discrimination-on-basis-of-gender-identity-or-sexual-orientation/.

Coates, Ta-Nehisi. *The Beautiful Struggle: A Father, Two Sons, and an Unlikely Road to Manhood*. Spiegel & Grau, 2009.

Comberg, David. "Kurt Vonnegut on the Shapes of Stories." *YouTube*. Uploaded 30 Oct. 2010. https://www.youtube.com/watch?v=oP3c1h8v2ZQ.

Delgado, Richard, and Jean Stefancic. *Critical Race Theory* (3rd ed): *An Introduction*. New York University Press, 2017. *ProQuest Ebook Central*. http://ebookcentral.proquest.com/lib/buffalo/detail.action?docID=4714300.

Ellwanger, Adam. "No Exit: White Speech and Silence in Classroom Conversations on Race." *Pedagogy: Critical Approaches to Teaching Literature, Language, Composition, and Culture*. Vol. 17, no. 1, 2017, pp. 35-58. doi: 10.1215/15314200-3658382.

Fight Club. Dir. David Fincher. Fox 2000 Pictures, 1999.

Foucault, Michel. "The History of Sexuality," *Literary Theory: An Anthology*, 2nd ed., edited by Julie Rivkin and Michael Ryan, Blackwell Publishing, 2004, pp. 892-99.

Freud, Sigmund. "The Uncanny." *Literary Theory: An Anthology*, 2nd ed., edited by Julie Rivkin and Michael Ryan, Blackwell Publishing, 2004, pp. 418-37.

Glover, Donald. "Childish Gambino - This Is America (Official Video)". *YouTube*. Uploaded 5 May 2018. https://www.youtube.com/watch?v=VYOjWnS4cMY.

Harris, Angela. "Foreword." *Critical Race Theory (*3rd ed.*): An Introduction*. Edited by Richard Delgado and Jean Stefancic. New York University Press, 2017, pp. 14-19. *ProQuest Ebook Central*. http://ebookcentral.proquest.com/lib/buffalo/detail.action?docID=4714300.

Hemingway, Ernest. "Hills Like White Elephants," *On Writing Short Stories*, 2 ed., edited by Tom Bailey, Oxford UP, 2011, pp. 180-84.

Horkeheimer, Max and Theodor Adorno. "The Culture Industry and Mass Deception." *Literary Theory: An Anthology*, 2nd ed., edited by Julie Rivkin and Michael Ryan, Blackwell Publishing, 2004, pp. 1242-46.

Kelly, Caroline. "Trump Bars 'Propaganda' Training Sessions on Race in Latest Overture to His Base." *CNN*, Cable News Network. 5 Sept. 2020. https://www.cnn.com/2020/09/04/politics/trump-administration-memo-race-training-ban/index.html.

Kennedy, John F. "Civil Rights Address." *American Rhetoric: Top 100 Speeches*. Delivered 11 June 1963. https://www.americanrhetoric.com/speeches/jfkcivilrights.htm.

Kincaid, Jamaica. *A Small Place*. 1988. Farrar, Straus and Giroux, 2000.

King, Stephen. "Premium Harmony." *The New Yorker*. 11 Nov. 2009. Conde Nast, 2018. https://www.newyorker.com/magazine/2009/11/09/premium-harmony.

Lamar, Kendrick. "Kendrick Lamar - HUMBLE." *YouTube*. Uploaded 30 Mar. 2017. https://www.youtube.com/watch?v=tvTRZJ-4EyI.

Morisson, Toni. *Beloved*. Vintage Books, 2004. 1987.

O'Connor, Flannery. "Everything that Rises Must Converge," *On Writing Short Stories*, 2nd ed., edited by Tom Bailey, Oxford UP, 2011, pp. 211-22.

Palahniuk, Chuck. *Adjustment Day*. W. W. Norton & Company, Inc., 2018.

——. *Fight Club*. 1996. W. W. Norton & Company, Inc., 2005.

——. "Not Chasing Amy." Uploaded 3 May 2009. https://www.imhd.nl/log/not-chasing-amy/.

——. "Stocking Stuffers: 13 Writing Tips from Chuck Palahniuk." *LitReactor*. 28 Nov. 2011. https://litreactor.com/essays/chuck-palahniuk/stocking-stuffers-13-writing-tips-from-chuck-palahniuk.

Riekki, Ron A. "Brandy, Shannon, Tender, and the Middle Finger: Althusser and Foucault in Palahniuk's Early Novels." Sartain. 89-101.

Rivkin, Julie and Michael Ryan. "Introduction: Strangers to Ourselves: Psychoanalysis." *Literary Theory: An Anthology*, 2nd ed., edited by Julie Rivkin and Michael Ryan, Blackwell Publishing, 2004, pp. 389-96.

——. Eds. *Literary Theory: An Anthology*. 2nd ed. Blackwell Publishing, 2004.

Sartain, Jeffrey A., ed. *Sacred and Immoral: On the Writings of Chuck Palahniuk*. Cambridge Scholars Publisher, 2009. ProQuest Ebook Central, http://ebookcentral.proquest.com/lib/buffalo/detail.action?docID=1114474.

Sheehan, Jason. "On 'Adjustment Day,' A Quick, Horrifying Descent into Madness." *NPR*. 1 May 2018. https://www.npr.org/2018/05/01/605000881/on-adjustment-day-a-quick-horrifying-descent-into-madness.

Street, Jon. "Biden Brings Back Critical Race Theory, Which Trump Called 'Divisive, Anti-American Propaganda.'" *Campus Reform*. Leadership Institute. 21 Jan. 2021. https://campusreform.org/article?id=16690.

Vonnegut, Kurt. *Breakfast of Champions*. 1973. Dial Press, 2011.

——. "Harrison Bergeron." *Welcome to the Monkey House*. 1968. Dial Press, 2014.

Chapter 4

"Another obsolete truth": Narrative and Construct in Chuck Palahniuk's *Rant*

Rebecca Warshofsky

State University of New York

Abstract: Transgressive fiction can be an effective tool in the literature classroom for promoting critical thinking because its characters clearly and frequently employ the same method of criticizing the world around them that any literature class aims to teach. In providing representations of social, moral, legal, and other types of boundaries and then subverting them to move beyond them by offering some alternative narrative, fictional portrayals of various transgressions highlight the arbitrary nature of *all* limits, suggesting that even "truths" that have the appearance of being eternal and unquestionable must be subject to scrutiny eventually. In this way, studying transgressive fiction can sharpen the critical eye by providing the occasion for understanding, analyzing, and reconceptualizing the functions of certain customs, traditions, habits, or assumptions that may be tacitly stagnating and subtly controlling various aspects of our experience. In particular, Chuck Palahniuk's *Rant: An Oral Biography of Buster Casey* demonstrates the process of deconstructing dominant narratives and reassessing the value of even the most implicit values. Through his absurd antics, the character Rant interrogates the relevance and efficacy of the structures that govern how we perceive and navigate our realities. Furthermore, Rant's behavior suggests that transgressing various societal conventions allows us to imagine and produce new possibilities for ways of thinking and being. After reading this text, undergraduate literature students have shown they can apply these processes of deconstructing narratives and revaluing values to real-world situations to come up with new interpretations of "truths" that they may have otherwise taken for granted.

Keywords: truth, narrative, construct, values, revaluation, critical thinking, transgressive fiction, subversion, morality, limits, boundaries, laws, conventions, tradition

***

"I want to ask, you ever wonder why the dominant culture says certain stuff?"

–Neddy Nelson, *Rant*

The question above is one about truth and power. It is the kind of question one can only ask if one has a critical enough eye to know that a question needs to be asked in the first place. It is a question that illuminates the distinction between knowing *what* to think and knowing *how* to think. This question is motivated by the understanding that the "stuff" the "dominant culture" says is not the only "stuff" it could say, and that analyzing *what* the "dominant culture" says ought to reveal something about *why* they are saying it. This is the connection between truth and power: that any narrative—that is, any coherent attempt at speaking a truth—implies a particular end, goal, purpose, desire, or drive, and that the speaker of said narrative—whether wittingly or unwittingly—promotes that end when they reproduce that narrative. So, in order to assess the value of any narrative that purports to say something true, we must ask: What is being said? Who is saying it? Why are they saying it (in the way that they are saying it)? What else might be said in its place, or in response to it? These are questions of critical thinking and critical analysis, and it seems not enough people in American society are asking them—as evidenced by anti-vaxxers, flat-earthers, QAnon supporters, Capitol rioters, COVID-deniers, and various other disbelievers of direct sensory experience—even though the ubiquity of technologies such as the internet and social media have made it so that humans are now confronted with more "truth" claims than ever before. This crisis of competing narratives can be mitigated and perhaps even overcome with a reliable method for distinguishing between narratives of different types, namely, those that are in line with the values they claim to promote, and those that are not. Part of telling the difference comes from being able to see that certain "truths" are perpetuated to accomplish certain ends—for instance, Trump perpetuated the narrative that he won the 2020 election not because he really won it, but because he wanted to remain in power. Thus, narratives like "Stop the Steal" and "Make America Great Again" are not in line with the values they claim to promote because they have their origins in Trump's and the Republican Party's hubris and greed rather than in the belief that there was some flaw in the 2020 election process or that Trump actually was the right person to bring about widespread, positive change in the U.S. In general, it should be easy to see through such narratives because the purposes behind them are so clear, due to the fact that the narratives and the entities perpetuating them are so easily identifiable with each other. In other words, understanding a narrative's meaning entails understanding the intentions that produced it.

Yet, as recent trends and the above events in the U.S., and others, have shown, it can still be very easy to be swayed by a narrative that is overtly pushing an agenda that does not align with the narrative itself.[1] If this is the case, then what is to be said for narratives for which one *cannot* see the purpose, especially because many individuals do not even realize that they are narratives in the first place since they have become so divorced from their original speaker or purpose? What about the more tacit narratives that subtly motivate people's behavior, like standards of beauty, gender norms, familial obligations, and notions of success? How can people learn to see what lies beneath the narratives they hear in order to decide which ones should shape their experience? That is to say: what might some *real* critical thinking look like in practice in society? What effects can it have? And how can students, let alone citizens, even tell when it needs to be employed in the first place? Learning to ask the right critical questions at the right times is the goal of any pedagogical practice that valorizes reading: it is what faculty are asking students to do when they encounter any text in any humanities class, and it is what we need more members of our society to do when they read (or hear) just about anything. To put it another way, wondering and asking about "why the dominant culture says certain stuff" is a skill that can and should be cultivated in literature classrooms to equip students with the tools to evaluate the various "truths" they encounter every day. Based on my experience teaching literature courses at the undergraduate level, one type of literature that works particularly well to promote this type of thinking is transgressive fiction because its characters clearly and frequently employ the same method of criticizing the world around them that a literature class aims to teach.

Teaching and Transgressive Fiction

Texts that fall under the label of "transgressive fiction" have a propensity to adopt a critical or mistrustful stance towards authority and the status quo,

---

[1] This includes but is not limited to: the Capitol riots that took place on January 6th, where hundreds of people used physical force to attempt to stop the certification of a legitimate election, believing then-President Trump's repeated, false claims that the election was stolen.

making them particularly well-positioned for presenting new interpretations of narratives, conventions, rules, and limits of various kinds. The characters of transgressive fiction tend to disregard normal, typical, required, or expected behavior in favor of more instinctual or authentic ways of being. To be transgressive means to transgress against *something*, so any work of transgressive fiction must necessarily present some formulation or understanding of the narrative, convention, rule, or limit that is being crossed, violated, or infringed. In providing representations of social, moral, legal, and other types of boundaries and then subverting them to move beyond them by offering some alternative interpretation, works of transgressive fiction show that narratives, conventions, rules, or limits are *constructed*—that is, built by humans—and thereby that they can be deconstructed. In this way, transgressive fiction furnishes the occasion for understanding and analyzing the function of certain "truths" and for investigating who is perpetuating which narrative and why. For instance, texts like Chuck Palahniuk's *Invisible Monsters* and *Fight Club* present the idea that standards of beauty for both women and men are propagated by corporations for profit, and that some path to fulfillment or self-realization might be found in the opposite of the "self-improvement" narrative—namely, in self-mutilation or self-destruction. Such examples demonstrate why transgressive fiction, in particular, can be a useful tool in the classroom to sharpen students' critical thinking skills: by portraying transgressions of various norms and expectations, these texts can both reveal narratives in places students did not expect them and demonstrate that it is possible to uncover alternative ways of thinking that run counter to the narratives they see and hear.

In his seminal volume of essays analyzing transgressive fiction, *Techniques of Subversion in Modern Literature: Transgression, Abjection, and the Carnivalesque*, M. Keith Booker defines the concept of transgression generally, as "the disruption of hierarchies, taxonomies, or limiting systems of all kinds" (Booker 12). Conceiving of transgression as a breakdown in the normal functioning of a system or a bending and fragmenting of its component parts is useful for conceptualizing what is taking place when characters act in ways that violate their culture's norms and expectations: the rule or boundary still exists and can even claim responsibility for cultivating the behavior that transgresses it, but the rule or boundary is being taken advantage of or applied in some way other than the purpose for which it was intended. This can have the effect of opening up a space where new meanings or ways of thinking can be produced—if the nature of a limit is to preclude *something* from being accessible, then it follows that transgressing a limit can grant access to some novel experience. Indeed, Booker notes that "Transgression and creativity have been inextricably linked throughout the history of Western culture," citing the story of Adam and Eve eating the forbidden fruit in the

Garden of Eden as the first transgression and therefore the very act that made the rest of human history possible (Booker 3). In the same way that an act of transgression can produce new meanings, a study of transgressive fiction can lend itself to changing the way one perceives or interprets the world. Booker writes, "[E]ven the most transgressive works of literature do not in general immediately send their readers into the streets carrying banners and shouting slogans. Transgressive fiction works more subtly, by gradually chipping away at certain modes of thinking that contribute to the perpetuation of oppressive political structures" (Booker 4). The phrase "modes of thinking" is vital here—the concept of transgression implies a new logic, one that goes beyond mere contradiction to liberate thought from dialectical constraints like history, morality, or even rationality.

Consider my student who, after spending a semester reading texts featuring transgressive acts, writes in her final paper:

> People are also inclined to believe something is true and right because it is tradition. "The Lottery"[2] by Shirley Jackson depicts a society that is stuck in their past ways, unable to modernize the way they think due to tradition. Without factual evidence, the community believes that truthfully, [killing one person per year via] the Lottery is the only way [for the community] to survive and thrive. They are unwilling to question whether it is fair, and this leads to innocent lives being taken away. […] Just like there has always been a lottery, for many individuals today, there has always been an electoral college. However, just because it is custom, is it truly fair? With the 2016 election people have been constantly questioning the idea of truth and tradition. Hillary Clinton surpassed Donald Trump with over 2 million popular votes, yet still lost due to the electoral college vote. The ritual where representatives from all states vote in the electoral college is likely corrupt.

Regardless of some imprecise language, this response is indicative of the shift in thinking that transgressive texts suggest through their examples of subversion. Considering the events of the story, the student understands the

---

[2] While this may not be a work that immediately comes to mind as an example of transgressive fiction, the character Tessie Hutchinson does attempt to commit a transgression against her society's fundamental rule that there must always be a Lottery, and this provides the occasion for analyzing the rule that is being transgressed. Plus, Shirley Jackson received a massive amount of hate mail for this story when it was first published—a sure sign that readers felt it had violated some sacred boundary!

character's attempt at transgression as the impetus for deconstructing a narrative; she then extends the logic of that call for transgression and deconstruction to a real-world situation. This particular instance of the student's analysis may not result in some radically new idea, but it represents a development in her thought process because it shows that she is paying attention to one of the hidden forces—namely, the very idea of tradition itself—that underlies the fundamental structure of the system in question, which in turn allows her to think about ways that system might be disrupted. This is just one example of how transgressive texts can erode the "modes of thinking that contribute to the perpetuation of oppressive political structures," as Booker contends (4). Furthermore, the "structures" that transgressive fiction can gradually change prevailing opinion on need not be exclusively political. As transgressive texts like Chuck Palahniuk's show, readers can interpret Booker's claim about "oppressive political structures" more broadly, as any hegemonic paradigm—"oppressive power structures" might be a more general way of saying it. For instance, consider how depictions of extreme sex acts in the work of Marquis de Sade paved the way for a more liberal public conception of sexual activity and sexual relationships. The transgression of a limit points out what the limit is; exceeding the limit is a reciprocal gesture in which actions that obey the limit are implied as they are negated at the same time, casting them in a new light and inverting their status as limit to erect new truths where the old ones once stood. This tendency towards iconoclasm and irreverence makes transgressive fiction appealing even to students who tend not to read because it inherently keeps readers guessing and allows them to see various aspects of the world from new perspectives. What follows is a case study of Chuck Palahniuk's *Rant: An Oral Biography of Buster Casey*, a text I have used in my classes to demonstrate to students the process of deconstructing narratives and reassessing the value of even the most implicit values. After reading this text, students have shown they can apply these processes to real-world situations to come up with new interpretations of "truths" that they had previously taken for granted as permanent and unchangeable facets of their experience.

Troubling Truths

Chuck Palahniuk's *Rant: An Oral Biography of Buster Casey* is a story in which small-town rebel, Buster "Rant" Casey, moves to the big city, joins a cult-like organization of demolition-derby drivers, spawns a rabies pandemic, and ultimately travels back in time in his perpetual attempt to "find something real in the world" (Palahniuk 60). To do all of this, he must call into question a variety of "truths" that characters and readers alike had previously taken for granted. Through his absurd antics, Rant demonstrates the type of thinking that any serious critical analyst or student of the humanities ought to be doing when they encounter various truth claims or narratives. This type of thinking interrogates the relevance and efficacy of the structures that produce human experience, and as such, it can offer new solutions to old problems—especially as they relate to tradition or traditional ways of thinking—because it attempts to look at a system from a perspective that is outside of that system. As a real-world example of this type of thinking, consider the shift that is taking place from conceiving of addiction as a crime to conceiving of it as a disease—it is easy to see how new solutions become possible in the context of this alternative, revaluated framework. In the same vein, by showing Rant's method of re-orienting himself toward his experience via the subversion of hegemonic value systems, Palahniuk's novel argues for the view that transgressing the conventions set up by society allows people to imagine and produce new possibilities for ways of thinking and being. Rant's behavior suggests that a narrative can be deconstructed and repurposed in the service of a different goal, and that the effects of putting new values, laws, or conventions in place of the old ones can be beneficial for individuals and communities alike. But in order to transgress the boundaries people encounter, they must first see them as boundaries, meaning they must first understand the nature of truth as constructed.

Even before it begins, *Rant* warns its readers of the slippery, perspectival, and contingent nature of truth. Readers are told: "This book is written in the style of an oral history, a form which requires interviewing a wide variety of witnesses and compiling their testimony. Anytime multiple sources are questioned about a shared experience, it's inevitable for them occasionally to contradict each other" (Palahniuk, "Author's Note"). Such occasional contradictions are present not only in oral histories, but in any history—such contradictions are at the heart of truth itself. Students compared the multiplicity of voices in *Rant* to the variety of media outlets where they access news—CNN, Fox, PBS, MSNBC—and were able to see how what purports to be "objectivity" is just another perspective, meaning that it is subject to error and revision. In other words, "truth" just happens to be the most agreed-upon narrative, but it is still a narrative. When a particular narrative has been agreed upon for long enough, people forget that it is a narrative at all—for instance, the existence of the Judeo-Christian God might be thought of in this way. The novel, *Rant*, appears in this "oral history" style to remind the reader of truth's constructed nature. The multiplicity of voices telling the story is a constant suggestion that "truth" is not the limit readers may have thought it was—it is not eternal unchanging; rather, it is dependent upon who is speaking and when. In class, students were able to use this conception of truth to deconstruct ideas like "success means achieving the American Dream" and "being a man means being physically and emotionally strong," among others.

For instance, after reading Palahniuk's *Invisible Monsters*, a text that critiques beauty standards and gender norms, one student wrote:

> Advertisements are filled with women and men posing and glorifying their bodies to sell some type of product whether it be makeup, gym memberships, or plastic surgery that'll make you look like them. If people can't live up to these standards, then they may see themselves as a failure, which is why Brandy [a main character] challenges who or what really should define the standards of beauty. For Brandy, an individual should create their own beauty by doing the opposite of what society wants....Beauty to Brandy, is finding an identity that one can be proud of even if it's not one that society expects of you.

Here, the student shows how understanding "truth" as a narrative that is constructed for a particular purpose means the truth can change, thereby placing less limitation on an individual's experience. Other iterations of this constructed conception of truth appear throughout *Rant*, such as Rant's friend Bodie Carlyle's assertion: "You can get plenty of folks telling the same lie if they got a stake in it. You get everybody telling the same lie and it ain't a lie, not no more" (Palahniuk 51). Similarly, Rant's fifth-grade teacher remarks: "In my classroom, I tried to impress on the students that reality is a consensus. Objects, from diamonds to bubble gum, only have value because we all agree they do. Laws like speed limits are only laws because most people agree to respect them" (Palahniuk 53-4). These conceptions of truth as "agreement" imply that the meaning or value of something *could have been other* than what it is—could *still be* other in the future. Meanings and values have histories that determine their status, histories that have particular inceptions and evolutions; an agreed-upon truth is therefore not a stagnant truth—it grows and changes as those who perpetuate it grow and change. Conversely, narratives can become dangerous and oppressive if they remain in place long enough to solidify and calcify. Rant leverages the very nature of truth by understanding it in this way, leading him to discover that it is possible to choose the direction in which certain narratives unfold—in other words, that "reality was something you could build" (Palahniuk 104). Because Rant is good at transgressing norms and revaluing values, the novel works well at helping students understand the significance of such actions and teaching students to spot occasions where they can employ these ways of thinking.

Manipulating Myths

To illustrate the sense in which a narrative evolves in terms of its meaning and applications, *Rant* provides several examples based on American culture: Santa Claus, the Easter Bunny, and the Tooth Fairy. These are useful examples to consider because the fact that they are narratives is clear—they are obviously constructed and therefore must be based on some purpose that inspired that construction. Furthermore, these examples show that even a narrative that is "patently invented and ludicrous" can have a tangible, palpable effect on one's experience, as Rant's friend Shot Dunyun elaborates: "Even the way a bizarre cultural delusion like Santa Claus can drive half of annual retail sales. Some mythological fat asswipe drives our national economy. It's beyond frustrating" (Palahniuk 130; 62). Rant understands that the purpose behind the narrative is much more real than the content of the narrative itself, and that this is the case, regardless of how "invented" the narrative appears. So, as a way of deconstructing them, Rant considers the original purposes of the narratives:

> By first believing in Santa Claus, then the Easter Bunny, then the Tooth Fairy, Rant Casey was recognizing that those myths are more than pretty stories and traditions to delight children. Or to modify behavior. Each of those three traditions asks a child to believe in the impossible in exchange for a reward. These are stepped-up tests to build a child's faith and imagination. The first test is to believe in a magical person, with toys as the reward. The second test is to trust in a magical animal, with candy as the reward. The last test is the most difficult, with the most abstract reward: To believe, trust in a flying fairy that will leave money. From a man to an animal to a fairy. From toys to candy to money. Thus, interestingly enough, transferring the magic of faith and trust from sparkling fairydom to clumsy, tarnished coins. From gossamer wings to nickels...dimes...and quarters. In this way, a child is stepped up to greater feats of imagination and faith as he or she matures. Beginning with Santa in infancy, and ending with the Tooth Fairy as the child acquires adult teeth. Or, plainly put, beginning with all the possibility of childhood, and ending with an absolute trust in the national currency. (Palahniuk 61-2)

On this view, the hidden value "absolute trust in the national currency" ends up being the original motivating factor behind the Tooth Fairy story—and behind the other two stories. Rant is able to reach this conclusion because he recognizes these narratives as narratives, enabling him to ask the questions "who is perpetuating this and why?" This destabilizes the narrative's limiting power, allowing him to imagine how to get beyond its original purpose, since the value of its original purpose is called into question after the narrative is deconstructed. Rant's next step is to repurpose the narrative so that it aligns with his own values, which allows him to obtain the effects he desires.

Rant uses the narrative of the Tooth Fairy to criticize the idea of the "absolute trust in the national currency" that shapes his life and the lives of those in his hometown of Middleton. Around the time he is in fifth grade, Rant clandestinely comes into possession of a huge collection of very old coins, each of which is worth thousands of dollars on average. To make his possession of the coins look less suspicious, Rant asks his friends to bring him their teeth in exchange for the coins and to tell their parents that they got the coins from the Tooth Fairy. The parents cannot question this reasoning without admitting they lied to their kids since the parents are the ones who perpetuated the Tooth Fairy story in the first place, regardless of whether they were ever aware of its original purpose. The kids begin to spend their Tooth Fairy money on whatever they want, leading to what Bodie Carlyle calls "the 'trickle-up' theory of prosperity. All the kids rich. All the adults smiling and wheedling and playing nice to get that money" (Palahniuk 53). Rant's actions subvert the whole idea of the "absolute trust in the national currency" because they put the financial power in the hands of the children instead of the adults—trust in the national currency cannot be "absolute" if the value of that trust is dependent on who has the currency. This vignette is an example of how a value ("absolute trust") gives rise to a custom or norm (adults control finances), which in turn gives rise to a narrative (Tooth Fairy) that then gets used to justify and perpetuate the "normal" behavior. After long enough, the narrative possesses the potential to become divorced from the original value (as demonstrated by Rant's scheme). In other words, the fact that Rant is able to use the Tooth Fairy story to undermine the original value on which it is based indicates that the value of that value needs to be reassessed. Rant harnesses this method of deconstructing and revaluing narratives for his own purposes to call into question and subvert a variety of limits throughout the novel—limits that are social, legal, and psychological, among others.

Rules of the Road

One such system that Rant criticizes through his actions is the traffic system. Humans invented this system, so it is clear that particular purposes and intentions inspired its construction. Furthermore, it is clear that the rules of the road were made up by people and therefore are not eternally binding in any significant way—it is not *impossible* to drive the wrong way down a one-way street, it is merely risky. On the surface, the traffic system may not look like a system that is necessary or worthwhile to transgress, but Rant views *any* system as an unwelcome limit on his experience. It is not the content of the system that is problematic for Rant; it is the simple fact that systems attempt to impose stability and therefore inhibit growth and change. While traffic laws appear to be based on values like order and safety, Rant and his friends see other purposes behind them. According to one of Rant's acquaintances, Green Taylor Simms, traffic laws "allow the maximum number of drivers to commingle on our roadways," meaning that the laws are surreptitiously motivated by the value of consumerism: by keeping the flow of traffic running smoothly, the laws allow more cars to fit on the road and to stay on the road for longer, causing more money to be spent on vehicles, parts, gas, maintenance, and accessories (Palahniuk 131). The monetary requirement imposed by the traffic laws also creates a hierarchy of status for those who partake in the system because more cars on the road means more varieties of cars being produced—everything from crappy clunkers driven by poor folks to souped-up sports cars driven by rich folks. In addition, the desire to keep those status symbols as pristine as possible requires drivers to stay far apart from each other, reducing opportunities for meaningful interactions with others. In a similar vein, Green observes that conforming to traffic laws implies "that the journey is always a means to some greater end, and the excitement and danger of the journey should be minimized. Perpetuating the fallacy that a journey itself is of little value" (Palahniuk 131). Conceiving of the traffic system as an arbitrary, constructed set of rules in service of an end they do not support triggers in Rant and his friends the impulse to transgress the limits the system imposes upon them in search of some more authentic way of being that is aligned with what they value.

Rant and his friends participate in an activity called Party Crashing. Party Crashing is a game where players join teams that drive around in cars looking for other participating cars to crash into. They only do this at night, but they use the very same roads that everyone else uses to go about their business during the day. By disregarding the traffic rules and using the system of roads in ways it was not intended to be used, Party Crashers subvert the rules of the road in order to get beyond them and establish new values. For instance, the impulse toward consumerism on which Rant believes the traffic system to be based gets inverted because in Party Crashing, cars with *more* dents and scratches are more coveted than ones that look shiny and new. Dents and scratches become symbols that mark veteran players who possess the wisdom of experience. In contrast to the way the traffic rules keep cars and the people in them apart from each other, Party Crashing brings people together in the cars themselves and imbues the journey itself with value as the people "sit around telling stories for a few hours...like a family" (Palahniuk 126-7). They also stop at gas stations to refuel and buy food, creating a whole "Pit-stop culture" where "teams come together and dissolve" in a "mingling, mixing party" with no rules or differentiations in status governing how the members of different teams interact (Palahniuk 208). In this way, Party Crashing ostensibly cancels out the social hierarchy that the traffic laws impose. In a letter to Bodie Carlyle, Rant describes how the game brings about this effect:

"[E]verybody being inside cars, you couldn't tell women from men. Black from white....The tough teams to beat were always the gimps. Gimps or queers. You put them in a car on a level playing field and you'd see some pent-up frustration. Nobody drove as hard as paraplegics with hand controls. Or skinny, hundred-pound girls" (Palahniuk 200). Here, the lack of structure imposed by the traffic system gives players the freedom to behave outside the norms and expectations of their culture due to the "level playing field" the game provides.

Similarly, Green describes an experience he has had while playing the game, which he refers to as "the piñata aspect" (Palahniuk 204). Instead of the experience of road rage that one might have while conforming to traffic rules,

> The joy [of Party Crashing] occurs when, with one nudge or scrape, that enemy vehicle bursts open to reveal stamp collectors, football fans, mothers, grandfathers, chimney sweeps, restaurant cooks, law clerks, ministers, teachers, ushers, ditch diggers, Unitarians, Teamsters, bowlers, human beings. Hidden inside that hard, polished paint and glass is another person just as soft and scared as you. (Palahniuk 204)

Categories and ways of classifying individuals retain no meaning or purpose because every identity is assigned the same status as "Party Crasher," or even just "human being." Furthermore, a car accident is a situation in which people expect to find feelings of indignation and resentment, but here the characters and readers find feelings of empathy instead. Because of all this, Green concludes that the community cultivated by Party Crashing "had been a form of consciousness-raising. Also, connection, dreaming, planning, perhaps even actual cultural change...a subculture that some [participants] have come to believe would have improved their quality of life" (Palahniuk 228-9). So, because the impulse for consumerism that produces all the rules and regulations of the traffic system has the hidden effect of forcing people into hierarchies, taxonomies, and the like, breaking the traffic rules leads to breaking down the limits that subtly and secretly control people's behavior by defining them and setting up expectations for them to conform to. Incredibly, transgressing against the traffic system by disregarding its established rules has the unanticipated effect of breaking down other social, economic, and cultural barriers that may not have previously appeared to be mutable, but are in fact only upheld by the antiquated values on which they are based.

Time to Transgress

As a final example of how Rant revalues narratives to suit his own purposes, he takes on the biggest, most abstract and seemingly permanent limit of all:

time itself. Rant's discovery of how to travel back in time is particularly significant pedagogically because it leverages the "fiction" aspect of transgressive fiction to allow students to think through what transgression means and how maintaining a psychologically open stance towards transgression can be valuable. With time travel, Palahniuk paints a picture of something readers understand to be physically impossible, which suggests that its significance in the context of transgressive fiction lies in readers' figurative or metaphorical interpretations of it.[3] Because of how Rant understands the truth, even limits such as the laws of physics are malleable: the physical laws of the universe can still be deconstructed and revalued because our perceptions of them come to us through narrative. To understand this, consider a case like Galileo's. Prevailing opinion was that the sun went around the Earth until Galileo's observations led him to claim that the reverse was the case; his claim was rejected because the Church wanted to continue to perpetuate the narrative that fit with their dominant paradigm and thereby served their purposes. The average citizen of Galileo's time had no reason to even question a physical law such as planetary motion in the first place. Analogously, Rant's criticism of physical laws asks readers and students to look for limiting narratives even in the places they least expect them. But in order to transcend time, there are other limits Rant must first overcome.

Rant's ability to transgress narratives, whose presence others do not even detect, comes from a lifetime spent cultivating his own worldview as freely of external influence as possible. A factor that contributes to this is that he grows up in a small town in the Midwest, at a distance from mainstream society. *Rant* takes place in a retro-futuristic version of the United States. The events it portrays occur sometime in the mid-1990s, but there exists a form of media technology called "boosted peaks," which Shot Dunyun describes as "the file record of somebody's neural transcript, a copy of all the sensory stimuli some witness collected," which can be downloaded and re-experienced by someone else via a port in the back of their neck (Palahniuk 114). Shot continues, "A port is like having an extra nose…only on the back of your neck. Only not just

---

[3] In other words, the fictional aspect of transgressive fiction allows students to notice opportunities for reinterpretation and revaluing in places they may not have seen them in reality, like my student who writes: "Chuck Palahniuk's unique writing style is able to make us question our society through the use of mutilation of the human body. This mutilation is not always in the sense of physical mutilation, but rather the destruction of the ideals in our society that are vital to human nature such as family and relationships….through the destruction of human bodies, Chuck Palahniuk's writing is able to 'destroy' our views about American culture as a whole. In other words, Palahniuk views the human body as a means for telling his view about our society and our ideals."

a nose, but eyes and a tongue and ears, five extra ways to see" (Palahniuk 146). With this technology, the user can witness an experience from the point of view of the original experiencer—like being a character inside a movie—so this technology has replaced other recorded media like TV and film in Rant's society. Users can also "boost" certain effects, like the experience of being on drugs, to enhance their own lived experience. In *Rant*, ports serve the same function that TV, film, and social media serve for us: they are the ultimate narrative-producing and narrative-perpetuating machine. Naturally, this has its downsides. According to Shot: "You're supposed to control a port, but sometimes you get a whole-body hunger for a Coke or potato chips, stuff you'd never eat, so you know the corporate world must broadcast peaks or effects that enter the port even when it's unplugged" (Palahniuk 146-7). But the motivation behind switching to the new media format is not just so that corporations can broadcast subliminal messages in the hope of selling more products. Boosted peaks end up playing a major role in shaping people's perceptions of reality by limiting how they experience time. In this sense, they can be viewed as a metaphor for the way the narratives people see and hear through media and culture affect them in ways they cannot even recognize or acknowledge. As it turns out, Rant is unable to use his port—it has been rendered inactive by the fact that he is infected with rabies.

Rant is single-handedly responsible for starting an enormous outbreak of rabies. He first contracts rabies while "fishing," an activity that consists of finding a hole in the ground and sticking a body part into it to see what kind of animal will bite him. He invents this activity after a random encounter with a black widow spider. Because the spider bit him but did not kill him, he considers himself "vaccinated against fear" and other kinds of "disease" like boredom, pain, and even death (Palahniuk 72; 69-70). Bodie Carlyle recounts: "Instead of boosting peaks, Rant wanted to go fishing. He used to say, 'My life might be little and boring, but at least it's mine—not some assembly-line, secondhand, hand-me-down life'" (Palahniuk 73-4). Rant also used to claim: "If you never been *rabid*, you ain't never lived" (Palahniuk 73). The fact that the practice of "fishing" entails only nature and the body is what allows Rant to associate having rabies with living and being alive: for Rant, "fishing" is an authentic practice because there is no narrative involved to turn his experiences into "secondhand, hand-me-down" experiences. In this way, spending time "fishing" instead of "boosting peaks" is what allows him to create his own narratives instead of having his identity fashioned for him by the culture and society in which he finds himself. If "rabies" is taken to be a metaphor for "a real, alive life," and "boosted peaks" are taken to be a metaphor for narrative in general, then having rabies ends up being Rant's "vaccination" against the effects of narrative itself (Palahniuk 300). In other words, because he shapes his own experience rather than letting it be shaped by the customs, laws, and limits he encounters, he cultivates a resistance to the external influences that were constructed to control people's behavior, allowing him to more easily recognize when a narrative needs revaluing.

One such constructed external influence is what appears to be the ultimate limiting narrative: that "[time] only moves in one direction" (Palahniuk 306). Rant figures out how to travel back in time, which he is only able to do because his port does not work (i.e., because he is not susceptible to the influence of dominant narratives), and his port does not work because he has rabies (i.e., because he replaces dominant narratives with his own). Rant's friend and fellow Party Crasher, Neddy Nelson, explains: "Isn't rabies what wrecks your port so you can't boost peaks? After that, aren't you free to flashback [in time]? [...] Isn't that why the government pushed to port everybody? Because weren't too many people [flashing back] to mess with history? [...] Don't you know about the covert government effect? People aren't even aware it's boosting, but doesn't the effect keep you stuck here so you can't mess with history?" (Palahniuk 279-280). Continuing to apply the metaphorical interpretations established above, we can take Neddy's observations to mean that certain narratives are perpetuated for the explicit purpose of ensuring that other, larger narratives will not be questioned. This is to say that if a narrative does not appear to be a narrative, it will not be subject to scrutiny and will thereby continue to be perpetuated. Rant and his friends theorize that the "time" narrative is perpetuated to keep people from going back in time to change history. In the novel this happens literally, but a useful metaphorical way of interpreting this is that the "time" narrative protects all other narratives from being questioned: figuratively "going back in time to change history" implies understanding history as a narrative—that it is constructed by people and perpetuated by people, and therefore that it is subject to change. If people share the consensus position that time "only moves in one direction," then they may view history as set in stone and not as the narrative it is, meaning it will not occur to them to question why it is presented the way it is or whether it can be presented differently, and one possible effect of this is that it keeps the perpetuators of historical narratives in power. To imagine the damaging effects of this view of history, consider as an example a history textbook that glosses over the horrors of slavery and thereby lays the groundwork for accepting racism by minimizing the struggles that Black people in the U.S. have faced and continue to face. Shot Dunyun poses the problem of the perception of time—which we are now interpreting as a metaphor for history or any hegemonic narrative—in the following way:

> Rant said once that you *perceive* time the way the people in power want you to. Like it's a speed limit on some freeway. Santa Claus or the Easter Bunny. Like time is the Tooth Fairy we're brought up to believe.

As a path or a river that only moves in one direction. But speed limits change. Santa Claus is fake. Rant told me that time's not the way we think. Time wraps. It loops. It stops and starts. And that's just the little bit he's found out. Most folks, Rant says, move through time like a flightless bird on land. Rant says that view of time was set up so folks won't live forever. It's the planned obsolescence we've all agreed to. (Palahniuk 306)

Once Rant figures out how to travel back in time, he is able to cultivate a super-human version of himself. Considering all of this metaphorically, it can be said that Rant's ability to overcome society's influences allows him to assert the meanings he created as the new limits that define what he is able to experience. Conversely, when a person tacitly agrees to a narrative because they never recognized it as a narrative, it can impose significant limits on their experience. Rant's car salesman, Wallace Boyer, explains this in another way: "If it helps, consider how people used to think the world was flat. Two-dimensional. They only believed in the part they could see, until somebody invented the ships and somebody brave sailed off to find the rest of the earth. Consider that Rant Casey is the Christopher Columbus of time travel" (Palahniuk 310). This is the sense in which we can consider Rant's time-traveling as a transgressive act that opens up the space for new possibilities to be created once the "truth" has been revalued. The main takeaway from Rant's experiences with time travel is that even though a particular narrative might appear to be harmless or might not appear to be a narrative at all, a consensus perception and tacit acceptance of it can have tangible effects on what is possible to experience. This insight calls for a more critical stance toward the very structures that produce and shape reality.

Putting a Point on Party Crashing Pedagogy

Interpreting Chuck Palahniuk's *Rant* literally would be a mistake. The text is not suggesting that time travel is possible or that it is a good idea to infect yourself with a disease or to go crash your car for fun. Instead, what these fictional events suggest is that hidden applications of power are all around, and knowing how to spot them and thereby transgress the limits they establish can allow students, as citizens, to navigate their experiences in ways they could never imagine—indeed, the novel contains many more transgressions and revaluations than just the ones mentioned here. This text—and transgressive fiction in general—suggests that approaching the world with a perspective that is critical of "truth" can allow individuals to discover authentic ways of being by pushing back against the narratives that shape experiences in ways people may never have noticed or agreed to.

However, it would also be a mistake to come away from this text with the impression that *no* narrative can ever be trusted and that *nothing* is true. To be critical of any narrative or truth claim is not the same thing as rejecting all narratives and truth claims outright. The critical stance that transgressive fiction texts suggest is a reminder that truths and the values that produce them ought to be in line with each other. Learning to identify which values underlie the truths people encounter entails figuring out *why* certain narratives became dominant in the first place, which means being critical of what purposes they serve and whether those purposes are still worth preserving. If they are not, individuals need to reorient their values so they can create new truths.

Another thing to note is that the transgressions Rant commits appear much more purposeful when everybody does them: Rant gets all the kids at his school to tell the Tooth Fairy lie, Party Crashing can only function with multiple teams, and rabies spreads throughout the population. This connects back to M. Keith Booker's claim that transgressive fiction can slowly chip away at the "modes of thinking" that perpetuate oppressive power structures—it turns the tide by involving more and more people over time. However, chipping away at harmful modes of thinking implies needing a first transgressor to point out an alternative way of thinking, doing, or being. This suggests teaching, cultivating, and promoting ways of thinking that allow students to see limits as constructed and thereby as able to be transgressed in the first place. Studying transgressive fiction can demonstrate what this type of thinking looks like because transgressive texts are predicated on an unwillingness to accept widely acknowledged truths as eternally binding or universally applicable. Analyzing any work of transgressive fiction has the capacity to promote the process of critical questioning by providing a framework for thinking through the various arbitrary restrictions cultures and societies impose, how they came to be, and how to get around them.

Failing to flex critical thinking muscles often enough can be downright dangerous. When left un-interrogated, beliefs and values can coalesce into dominant narratives, which, in turn, can become codified in the form of social norms and even institutions. When a value becomes monolithic, and its origin is obfuscated, repressed, or forgotten, it can start to do some serious harm to the people who did not create it and to whom it was never meant to apply. Therefore, every so often, the value of even the most tacitly accepted values must itself come under scrutiny. If the value of a specific value is never scrutinized or criticized, the culture containing it can end up producing radicals and extremists because believing in any one thing for too long makes believers forget that other ways of thinking, feeling, doing, and being are possible, acceptable, and even useful. However, real-world examples of transgressions and disruptions to hegemonic systems are happening all the time—anything from Rosa Parks's refusal to give up her seat on a segregated bus to the group of Redditors who bought enough stock in Game Stop to throw the stock market out of whack. Analyzing these types of events points out weaknesses in the systems of which they are a part, thereby creating the space for change to take place. In this way, transgression is the logic the propels the process of revaluation. Transgressive fiction suggests perpetual growth and change as the best method for bringing about new alternatives for engaging with the world and for promoting authentic experience. But to engender that growth and change, it must be possible to think in a way that can bring such change about.

Teaching students critical thinking skills is—or at least should be—one of the main goals of any humanities class. Texts like Palahniuk's work well for teaching these skills because they demonstrate instances of what critical thinking looks like by interrogating aspects of society that may not have appeared to need interrogating in the first place. In this way, reading transgressive fiction can serve to highlight the importance of moving beyond traditionally accepted ways of thinking and being. Once students understand truth as constructed in the way *Rant* presents, they are more inclined to notice the dangers in making assumptions about the necessity of upholding various customs, traditions, conventions, and structures; this way of thinking can prevent harmful or oppressive ideas from taking root, spreading, and becoming a basis on which to build further uncritical ideas. After my class read *Rant*, students wrote claims like "Transgression plays an important role in society as it allows for progression and limits the stagnation of ideas," and "Transgression…is a necessary step for moving humanity forward. By straying from the accepted customs of everyday life…positive changes result for mankind." Texts like *Rant* show that transgression is possible precisely because the limits that various "truths" appeared to present are in fact changeable and that changing them becomes necessary when they no longer represent what people value. Transgressive fiction can allow students to see what society looks like through a critical lens and thereby equip students with the tools to apply this lens themselves.

Studying transgressive fiction is about learning to ask the right questions. In general, people in American society are not asking the right questions because reality is being presented to them in such a way as to preclude the possibility of questioning from even arising. Simply put, individuals must be equipped with the skills to tell for themselves when "fake news" is actually fake. Transgressive fiction can teach how to trace the lineage of a narrative through power by demonstrating the point at which that power breaks down; people must learn to apply this skill of criticizing narratives consistently, regardless of whether the narrative is "Make America Great Again" or "Black Lives Matter." Transgressive fiction can teach this skill by demonstrating a particular understanding of what truth is and how it functions, which can then be applied to the world in order to revalue the narratives that shape experience. Chuck Palahniuk's *Rant: An Oral Biography of Buster Casey* shows what is to be gained from taking this critical stance toward reality. This type of critical thinking must become more widespread if profound, structural, and even revolutionary change is to occur in the way people engage with each other and in the way society functions.

Works Cited

Booker, M. Keith. *Techniques of Subversion in Modern Literature: Transgression, Abjection, and the Carnivalesque.* University of Florida Press, 1991.

Jackson, Shirley. "The Lottery." 2005. PDF.

Palahniuk, Chuck. *Fight Club.* W.W. Norton & Company, Inc., 1996.

Palahniuk, Chuck. *Invisible Monsters.* W.W. Norton & Company, Inc., 1999.

Palahniuk, Chuck. *Rant: An Oral Biography of Buster Casey.* Anchor Books, 2007.

Further Reading

Foucault, Michel. "A Preface to Transgression." *Language, Counter-Memory, Practice: Selected Essays and Interviews,* edited by Donald Bouchard, Cornell University Press, 1977, pp. 29-52.

Hume, Kathryn. *Aggressive Fictions: Reading the Contemporary American Novel.* Cornell UP, 2012.

Jenks, Chris. *Transgression.* Routledge, 2003.

Mookerjee, Robin. *Transgressive Fiction: The New Satiric Tradition.* Palgrave Macmillan, 2013.

Nietzsche, Friedrich. *Beyond Good and Evil/On the Genealogy of Morality.* Edited by Alan D. Schrift and Duncan Large. Stanford University Press, 2014.

Stallybrass, Peter and Allon White. *The Politics and Poetics of Transgression.* Cornell. University Press, 1986.

Chapter 5

The Laughter of the Dead: Theorizing Noise, Trauma, and Incantation in Palahniuk's *Lullaby*

Josh Grant-Young

University of Guelph

Abstract: In a world inundated with noise, "it would be nice to see words come back into power" *Lullaby's* Carl Streator notes in relation to the power of the "culling song" - an incantation with the power to kill anyone it is read to. Palahniuk's *Lullaby* is, on its surface, the tale of a road trip to destroy every copy of *Poems and Rhymes Around the World*, an anthology which contains such a culling song with mortal ramifications for any who hear it. Lullabies, like the one above, are meant to ease the traumatic noise which pollute the home and put the traumatized to rest. Whether one considers the primary characters of the story, haunted houses, the parents of dead infants who Streator (a journalist) interacts with, or the author himself, *Lullaby* seeks meaning in silence (in relation to violent noise) and incantation to put to rest the spectres of noise in our contemporary condition. Drawing on philosophy, media studies, psychotherapy and ancient lullabies, this chapter will explore the occult "power of words" to ease trauma in an age of mass media and violence, to sooth not only the cradle but set right the house entire. *Lullaby* problematizes both the soothing capacity of words as means to bring silence and closure to traumatic episodes, and the very notion of closure itself in death (the ultimate silence). Such efforts prompt several questions: How might *Lullaby* productively complicate our cultural attitudes towards trauma? Do we, as a culture, place a problematic amount of importance of the search for closure? Is silence, in a world of noise, ever achievable (or desirable)?

Keywords: Lullaby, Chuck Palahniuk, Trauma, Noise

***

> The muffled thunder of dialogue comes through the walls, then a chorus of laughter. Then more thunder. Most of the laugh tracks on television were recorded in the early 1950's. These days, most of the people you hear laughing are dead… The stomp and stomp and stomp of a drum comes down through the ceiling. The rhythm changes. Maybe the beat crowds together, faster, or it spreads out, slower, but it doesn't stop. Up through the floor, someone's barking the words to a song. These people who need their television or stereo or radio playing all the time. These people are so scared of silence. These are my neighbours. These sound-oholics. These quiet-ophobics. Laughter of the dead comes through every wall. These days, this is what passes for home sweet home…
>
> – Carl, *Lullaby* (2002)

When is the last time you enjoyed silence?

People live in a world of noise – loud, abrasive, thundering noise. The media they consume, the sounds inside and outside their houses, on the daily commute to work, and the last things they hear before bed. This is the primary insight of protagonist Carl Streator's cultural critique in chapter three of Chuck Palahniuk's *Lullaby* (2002): we live in a world devoid of silence. Few spaces, if any, are not saturated with noise.

Within this chapter, I focus on three connected themes and their application for students exploring trauma in literature: the role of silence in such a world of noise, the presence of trauma within the narratives of Palahniuk's work, and the magic and incantations found in lullabies themselves – seeking to silence the traumatic power of noise. The marriage of these three themes is a recurring set of questions posited by this chapter: why might Carl (or Palahniuk, or even readers sympathetic to Carl's worldview) seek silence in place of noise? What can silence offer us as an alternative (for example, to trauma)? Can the act of silencing be understood as transgressive or moralistic? The structure of the chapter, then, might be best understood as three meditations on silence in a thunderous world of noise.

In the chapter, I attend to the pedagogical value of *Lullaby*, proposing several valuable insights one might glean as a reader. Chiefly, teaching Palahniuk along with trauma narratives can present students with the opportunity to reflect on what a trauma narrative—even employed through the realm of fiction—can be. Further, regarding lullabies themselves, students might find *Lullaby* enriching or complicating their notion of what is said over the crib – its function, content, and magical qualities found in the "power of words." At various junctures, I also offer reflective questions or suggestions for writing assignments geared towards student interpretation of the novel. In most cases, I consider how engagement with wider literature might aid in alternative interpretation of the novel itself, or chief characters like Carl. However, in a later section devoted to assessing various lullabies and culling songs found around the world, I suggest that one pedagogical method might include the speculative writing of culling songs themselves, allowing students to investigate a proposed analysis of the function of lullabies.

A key difference between this chapter and other work on *Lullaby* and Palahniuk's wider corpus (and of interest to this volume) is found in the theme of transgression. *Lullaby* is, like many of Palahniuk's works, touted as a critique of Western contemporary culture and media saturation (Keesey 51). Yet, while one might laud this rejection of the culture as radically oriented, pointing towards something fundamentally wrong in our noisy world, the solutions provided by characters within *Lullaby* ought to give us pause. Silence, if one takes this social critique as the dominant means by which to read *Lullaby*, is not a gesture of liberation from our culture, but rather an effort to shift control to other (admittedly more moralistic or reactionary) hands.

But what if, instead of the focus on media culture, students could consider the employment of silence and noise through trauma theory, seeing the desire to control as not another side of a political coin, but a trauma response to reclaim one's own life and words in a world where one's suffering has been silenced? Exploring themes of trauma found in *Lullaby* and other works of Palahniuk's corpus, offer a re-reading of *Lullaby* as a Gothic trauma narrative that, in side-stepping concerns over media mind control, represents efforts to find relief from the forces of trauma in an individual's life. Silence here is framed, through an analysis of Carl's character, as an ability to regain control over one's condition in a world where "no one's mind is their own" (Palahniuk 19). Noise, conversely, is explored through the employment of narrative unreliability, a common Gothic trope, which is utilized with many of Palahniuk's works.

How might lullabies, then, be understood differently on this account? By engaging with real lullabies and "culling songs" found across the world, this chapter works to "return words to power"—as Carl hopes they might be—by focusing on the magical roots of the function of the lullaby. Despite the potential for secular themes and content, lullabies have an ancient history and a magic reparative purpose: to quiet not simply the crib but the very cosmic trauma of noise itself. Assessing lullabies from ancient Babylon, as well as Albanian, Ainu and Finnish sources, like magic itself, lullabies follow a formulaic and reparative logic designed to bring peace to both the domestic and world at large.

Lullaby, then, represents a novel with significant ties to various fields: trauma studies, Gothic horror, and the anthropology of music and religion. Palahniuk's text is a rich mediation that moves beyond mere social critique of media, opening itself to a wider set of interpretive frameworks that can be explored in an interdisciplinary setting to meet the challenge of a world saturated by sound. Further, in complicating preconceptions of the radical nature of transgression, *Lullaby* re-read might instead provide a restorative narrative for confronting trauma, giving its protagonist an avenue out of self-destruction and paranoia.

Truly Transgressive? Silence's Moralism and Reactionary Elements in *Lullaby*

Is transgression always a liberatory gesture, or can the shirking of cultural norms and practices also breed a certain reactionary politics? Various critics have noted *Lullaby* is a novel well-situated within the general theme of transgressive social critique of Palahniuk's work.[1] After all, many of Palahniuk's best-known works are often tales of outsiders trying to, in novel and bizarre fashion, escape the demands and stringent rules of a hypocritical and fundamentally messed-up culture. Palahniuk's works are often understood as transgressive works of fiction, ones which playfully employ various social taboos, challenge convention, and even provoke fear and disgust within readers. But is *Lullaby* truly a challenge to the status-quo, or an affirmation of a different approach to control itself?

This generalized theoretical position, which I term the "social critique" reading of Palahniuk's work, is not without substantial truth. I make no claims here to suggest its falsity. However, I question its utility as a pervasive means by which to make sense of Palahniuk's contribution to transgressive literature—that this ought to be the dominant means by which to read Palahniuk as a critic of our morally bankrupt Western culture. I open this section with a provocative counter to such a transgressive picture of *Lullaby*'s protagonists—chiefly to problematize the transgressive nature of the text, suggesting there is greater nuance worth exploring.

In this section, I prod this "social critique" reading of Palahniuk, suggesting that *Lullaby*'s characters, rather than serving as transgressive heroes who push

---

[1] For (a non-exhaustive list of) examples of various reviewers, scholars and critics who note Palahniuk's social criticism as a foundational principle of his transgressive credibility, see: Green (2002); Keesey (2016); McCracken (2020); Mendieta (2005); Ziegler (2007).

the boundaries of the rational and sane within our culture, might well be understood as moralistic and reactionary in outlook. Though I will later dismiss many of these concerns in favor of a more nuanced and multi-perspectival reading of the text, I primarily aim to complicate the "social critique" reading of Palahniuk as a one-dimensional approach which takes transgression as a given liberatory gesture.

Silence, Control, and the Power of Words

This isn't about love and hate ... It's about control. People don't sit down and read a poem to kill their child. They just want the child to sleep. *They just want to dominate.* No matter how much you love someone, you still want to have it your own way. (emphasis my own)

– Helen, *Lullaby* (148)

A theme within *Lullaby* which has received some minor discussion is the power of words and silence to control or dominate others. Carl, in his more paranoid moments in the text, often refers to the noisy world of "Big Brother," constantly saturating culture with all manner of messages aimed at manipulating civilian minds. Certainly, such a sentiment seems quite in line with a transgressive social criticism like that of Keesey who suggested Palahniuk is pointing towards culture as one steeped in "corporate attempts to control consciousness" (Keesey 51).

But can one truly say that the desire for silence is a transgressive one in this novel? On a superficial level, *Lullaby* certainly foregrounds the struggle against a world saturated by media nonsense and noise, but the methods by which the protagonist and his motley crew resist "Big Brother" seem rather reactionary or moralistic by comparison. As I will discuss, the idealization of silence that Carl and Oyster take up within *Lullaby* is better framed as a series of conservative gestures, looking to return either to some primordial silence or force ecologically primitivist values onto the world.

If the transgressive anti-heroes within the book aim to challenge the status-quo of a culture, their choice of utilizing the grimoire, a spell book or magical "manual" of spells (traditionally for returning the dead to life, controlling others, or invoking demons or other spirits) seems an odd counter to media control. One argument for Helen's thesis of domination found within the quote above is the speculative contents of the grimoire's contents. Aside from the culling song, readers are presented with a "love" spell employed to exert control over others and an "occupation spell," one which allows the speaker to inhabit and dominate other bodies. The grimoire, it seems, is not at all a benign force in the world but contains at least three spells (culling, love and occupation) that aim to manipulate those around the reader: to silence (or, in certain hands, kill), and to control.

Oyster, as readers might expect (if they had shared the suspicions that Carl had for much of the novel), steals the sole copy and spends the latter part of *Lullaby* using the grimoire to advance his eco-terrorist views. He also employs the occupation spell to try to kill Helen (occupying her and forcing her to commit suicide – though she uses the same spell at a crucial moment to take a new form) (Palahniuk 252-255). Oyster's use of the grimoire, like his efforts to produce numerous class action lawsuits to disrupt capitalism, is a moralistic use of language to silence and manipulate/dominate others. The silence he wishes to bring to the world is one which reflects his own twisted conception of reality, showing that the magic within the grimoire is by no means neutral in application. For Oyster, the grimoire can be used in righteous judgment of the ecological and economic sins of contemporary capitalist culture – a chance for "wiping the slate clean" found in the destruction of humanity (Palahniuk 161).

One might even interpret Carl's own efforts to silence the world of noise around him as problematizing the radical nature of silence. Throughout *Lullaby*, Carl becomes a serial killer: various persons who annoy or offend him are unceremoniously killed with the culling song. Many of Carl's pronouncements regarding the power of the culling song admonish the culture around him and the need for an end to the "arms race of sound"—the "quiet-phobics" and "sound-oholics" are not to be sympathized with, but actively despised for their slavish love of noise (Palahniuk 17). Carl's rants and misgivings about "Big Brother" and the proliferation of noise seem more about having his 'own way' than any desire to implement some manner of transgressive silence. Carl merely wants the world to shut up for him – to return to a primordial silence that invokes book burnings, censorship, and killing words that leave only the "deaf" and "illiterate" unharmed (Palahniuk 42; 43).

If readers or students were to simply accept the social critique reading of *Lullaby*, they would be presented with characters who are, frankly, manipulative and practically irredeemable pricks. There seems to be, in this account, little to rescue them from their advocacy of reactionary desires to silence the world and destroy any element of culture which does not correspond to their conception of morality or desires. Their methods are suspect, and the goals they wish to achieve thoroughly nihilistic. If humanity refuses to better itself (by ending its role in ecocide – for Oyster- or divorcing itself from its slavish love of television and all things noisy – for Carl), then its extinction is justified. Transgression, here, seems to be a mere stand-in term for reprehensible political views which readers might find altogether unsympathetic.[2]

For readers or students who might, by this point, be dissuaded from finding any redeemable qualities within Carl, I suggest this is not the sole way to read the novel (or even other Palahniuk novels). Rather, by diving deeper into the context of *Lullaby*'s publication and its engagement with horror (particularly Gothic horror), students might find a greater appreciation for the otherwise unexplained eccentricities of Carl. In a classroom setting, one might explore the roots of Carl's behavior within trauma, applying both psychological literature and trauma theory to better grasp why Carl's reactions to noise are not simply a critique of our media-inundated culture, but a traumatic response worthy of another mode of interpretive analysis.

Trauma Narratives and the Importance of Trauma for Palahniuk's Work

In this chapter, I wish to present an alternative reading of the novel, drawing in part from existing literature on the confluence of Palahniuk's transition into horror as a medium and trauma as an undercurrent within Palahniuk's broader corpus. This is not to say I disagree fundamentally with the media-driven message of *Lullaby* that author and critics have established consensus on—there is much to mine there—rather, I suggest there is something pedagogically valuable about the marriage of horror and trauma narratives found in an alternative critical vantage point.

Why trauma? Palahniuk's life had, prior to the publication of *Lullaby*, taken a dark turn with the murder of his father, Fred. Fred had been dating a woman named Donna Fontaine (they had met through a personal ad), not knowing that Fontaine's former partner Dale Shackleford (in prison for sexual abuse) intended to, upon release, murder Fontaine. Following his release, Shackleford stalked the pair on a date and murdered them at Fontaine's residence. In interviews, Palahniuk suggested that writing *Lullaby* was a coping mechanism for this traumatic event and his decision to be a part of the process to determine whether Shackleford ought to receive the death penalty (Willis).

---

[2] Douglas Keesey notes that, in discussing issues of censorship, power and mass media, that Palahniuk himself may well have written these characters aware of the reactionary implications of their view and contradictory elements of their struggle against power via methods of control and censorship, though this is mentioned primarily in passing rather than subject to considerable scrutiny in his writing on *Lullaby*.

Further, trauma has often bled into the social critiques of Palahniuk, a factor deserving of commentary. Many of the characters of Palahniuk's novels experience forms of trauma which shape their narrative arc, often informing or acting alongside cultural critique. In her chapter "Trauma, Gender, and Commodification in Chuck Palahniuk's *Fight Club* and *Invisible Monsters*" (2002), Laurie Vickroy writes:

> With a postmodern sensibility and in a uniquely black humorous tone, Chuck Palahniuk tackles multiple familial and cultural contexts of trauma. He unveils stories of contemporary life through characters with chaotic lives and topical symptom formations of self-mutilation, self-medication, and support-group participation. Postmodernly irreverent and entertaining, his emotionally numb characters provide readers some emotional distance from traumatic material… Palahniuk walks a fine line in combining painful loss with the absurd ways his characters try to cope. Similar to the postmodernists Kurt Vonnegut and Joseph Heller, he creates tensions between tragic realism and fictionalization, and between trauma and absurdity, in the service of social satire. (154)

However, I will demonstrate, the influence of trauma goes beyond mere cultural critique in *Lullaby*. Rather, *Lullaby* represents a reckoning with trauma through the formulation of narrative through the role of a traumatized subject as narrator. Narration, on an account informed by trauma theory, allows such a subject to make meaning of events related to their trauma and the source of the trauma itself, in some manner reconstructing aspects of a shattered identity. As much as *Lullaby* might continue aspects of Palahniuk's social criticism, it also reflects a continued trend in his work to explore traumatized subjects and their efforts to make sense of their lives in the wake of devastating events. Thus, this chapter shifts the focus away from social criticism towards trauma, arguing there are equally valid and rich means of interpretation beyond the former (Collado-Rodríguez 625).

Finally, Palahniuk's shift to horror in a trilogy of works (*Lullaby*, *Diary*, and *Haunted*) mark an engagement with the Gothic horror genre, one steeped in traumatic narratives. Collado-Rodríguez considers this shift important as it unsettles the boundaries between the real and supernatural, eschewing more familiar readings of the Gothic within Palahniuk serving a political purpose.[3] However, while Collado-Rodríguez's work is instructive, I wish to engage more deeply with both trauma and the Gothic.

One example of a Gothic trope absent in Collado-Rodríguez's reading of *Lullaby* is the "Gothic loop." An important aspect of Gothic fiction is the narrative propensity towards "retrospective, repetitive, or circular" modes of storytelling, where time and past events are often looping back on themselves. Personal crisis, loss, and events are often relived by the protagonist, experiencing again and again their "forceful intrusion" in one's life (Juranovsky 1). Andrea Juranovsky writes the following concerning the "Gothic loop":

> the Gothic loop could be defined as a discursive element, a fictional time and space of various suspensions when/where certain past or present traumas must be continuously re-experienced and finally resolved—with horror and suffering involved on the part of the protagonists—in order to produce an improved (re)starting point in the narrative. Within the frame of the Gothic loop a previously repressed event of the past suddenly imposes itself upon the present and refuses to leave in an attempt to haunt the minds of the protagonists until they submit to face the challenge which the processing of that past memory has to offer. (1)

In *Lullaby*, I argue, this "Gothic loop" is indeed at work within the novel, particularly affecting the life of Carl. Carl's journey across the American landscape to destroy every copy of *Poems and Rhymes Around the World* pushes him to repeatedly face the source of his trauma. Carl remains haunted by his past in *Lullaby*, unwilling to forgive himself for the accidental death of his wife and daughter (from his reading of the culling song) and constantly finding himself uttering the same fatal words (or merely thinking them), re-experiencing his trauma again and again. Whether he is able, by the end of the novel, to reach some redemptive arc or at least an "improved (re)starting point," will be discussed later in the chapter.

---

[3] Collado – Rodríguez portrays the Gothic as a literary genre of "social subversion," which has prompted discussion in literature surrounding *Lullaby* to focus less on the Gothic in relation to fantastic elements of the novel and more directly on "the book as a metaphoric strategy aimed at different political meanings. Collado – Rodríguez notes Peter Matthews' (2009) suggestion that *Lullaby* explores "the difference existing in language between what is legal and what is moral," and Lance Rubin's (2008) reflection on the "political and moral effects of 9/11 and the risks of portraying explicit manifestations of terrorism, as Palahniuk has done in previous fiction…".

"... [w]e're all of us haunted and haunting...": Trauma and *Lullaby*

How do we tell stories about trauma? Where to begin? Or take control of our story? Trauma is difficult to put to paper because the process of working through and reclaiming one's narrative is filled with various challenges and potential pitfalls. Confronting troubling memories or piecing together foggy fragments, resurrecting suppressed details–by no means is it a pleasant experience in many cases. This section of the chapters seeks to frame *Lullaby* in relation to trauma narratives, arguing there is much which draws these forms of writing together in a productive manner.

Collado-Rodríguez notes a contemporaneous genesis shared by Palahniuk's literary career and that of the scholarly field of Trauma Studies. This connection is by no means superficial, Collado-Rodríguez argues, as both Trauma Studies and works like *Lullaby* share a similar "recognition of a negative aspect affecting the human being" – that the individual under scrutiny is a "victim of a psychic (and often also physical) injury" (Collado-Rodríguez 625). Collado-Rodríguez argues that Carl is "severely traumatized," blaming himself for the death of his wife and daughter, a deep wound which he wrestles with throughout *Lullaby* and binds him to Helen (who also lost her family).

Though Carl's traumatic backstory does not necessarily excuse his actions as a serial-killer in *Lullaby*, it certainly puts things in a more nuanced and helpful perspective than a straight-ahead reading of Carl as a social-critic-turned-killer. Carl's psyche is fragile, and he is someone who is quickly revealed as having a difficult time coping with the world around him and the feeling of responsibility for the death of his family. In expanding on Carl's psychological condition, I hope to account more accurately for what ails him and provide some guidance on how *Lullaby* might be a reparative, rather than nihilistic, narrative. Students in literature classes might, in such a context, consider how trauma theories and psychological literature present Carl's psyche not as disaffected or reactionary, but rather delve into his symptoms and expressions as a means to better understand how trauma informs his fragile world-view.

Getting the World to Shut Up for a Second: PTSD and Noise

This chapter opens with a lengthy passage from the third chapter of *Lullaby*, where Carl bemoans the sound-saturated apartment complex in which he lives. Neighbors play music and watch television at exceedingly high volumes, any tenant's nightmare. But there is something unique about Carl's ambivalence towards noise that sets his desire for silence apart from the average person's: post-traumatic-stress-disorder (PTSD) (Palumbo et al.; Siepsiak et al.)

Certain sounds, which seem innocuous to the average person, are capable of triggering memories of traumatic events or affecting the day-to-day life of those who experience PTSD in profoundly different ways. *Phonophobia* (the fear of sound), *misophonia* (aversion to sounds – particularly ones associated with traumas), and *hyperacusis* (a generalized reaction to tolerance / volume of sounds) are various reactions to noise that can be found among (though admittedly with varying frequency) individuals with PTSD.

PTSD is one of the most common diagnoses linked to misophonia (Rouw and Erfanian 456). Misophonia often finds its genesis in childhood or adolescence, qualified by an "intense negative emotional reaction is usually triggered by bodily sounds (e.g., chewing, breathing, swallowing, and foot tapping, etc.) and may be connected to a particular person creating that sound" (Palumbo et al. 2). Along with emotional reactions, those who experience misophonia occasionally report "physical pressure building in the chest, the desire to stop the person from making the sound, and other autonomic reactions" (Palumbo et al. 2). Often, because individuals with misophonia are unaware of when the trigger sound for their condition might present itself, they wait "in a perpetual state of anxiety" and avoid a variety of situations, individuals, and other things which might cause the triggering sound (Palumbo et al. 2).

Hyperacusis, though a rare occurrence, is nonetheless of interest here. For individuals experiencing hyperacusis, their toleration of sounds differs greatly from those who do not, as hyperacusis makes everyday noises seem too loud when others do not experience them as such. Rather than specific sounds (as in the case of misophonia), hyperacusis tends to refer to an aversion to sounds in general. As a result, one's ability to function in various environments inside and outside the home are compromised to varying degrees, and an increase in anxiety or fear often accompanies the experience of hyperacusis (Baguley). Drawing these various responses to noise, we might now ask where Carl falls within these aversions to noise. Hyperacusis seems far more likely, as Carl is not triggered by a specific sound, but rather an ever-present ecology of noise. He certainly identifies key culprits like television sets, loud talking, and animals. Yet, no one stands out from the others. Baguely notes that often a primary response to episodes is to "protect themselves with ear plugs, muffs or other devices." Certainly, there is a level of avoidance which Carl engages in which seems typical to issues with misophonia, but again, this is also true of hyperacusis.

However, while students might be quick to diagnose Carl as suffering from hyperacusis, it is worthwhile to consider this phenomenon within a narrative context as well, looking to literary forms of noise found in narrative unreliability, a common aspect of Palahniuk's work.

Complicated / Unreliable Narratives: Another Type of Noise

Though authorial intent might very well be focused on a critique of the noise pollution contemporary culture faces daily, it is curious that Palahniuk employs the symptomology of various psychological aversions to noise in *Lullaby* – so much so that it seems more than mere coincidence. Agreeing with Collado-Rodríguez, one can't help but infer that Carl exists in a state of psychic injury and that the noise which Carl avoids, and laments, is indeed indicative of some post-traumatic stress. His acting out against noise or even murderous rages are predicated on interacting with noise. Here, astute students might investigate the text to determine what trauma has placed Carl in such an unenviable position?

A challenge in determining a clean answer is the narrative unreliability of Carl, a point where Collado-Rodríguez and Vickroy agree. Between temporal hopscotch, half-truths, fragmented identities and hidden details, Palahniuk's protagonists are not only hard to pin down, but more than willing to refuse or suppress key details of their inner lives. The pair also agree, this unreliability comes, in part, from the traumatic subjectivity of Palahniuk's characters, who are often (like some real trauma sufferers) subject to memory and identity fragmentation, because of past traumas. Students familiar with his earlier works, *Fight Club* in particular, might examine how memory and the fracturing of identity function across Palahniuk's works, drawing on scholars like Vickroy for guidance in interpretative efforts.

Narrative unreliability, I suggest, is another type of noise that lies humming beneath the narrative of *Lullaby*. Though Kevin Stevens notes in his work on narrative unreliability that noise has no singular purpose that can be generalized across literature, some frequent trends emerge. Noise can act as a force that dissembles and transgresses boundaries, create chaos in an ordered world, or unearth elements of a character's life or information they wish to obscure (Stevens 202-204). For Carl, it seems every time he finds himself surrounded by noise, we get a deeper look into his damaged psyche, seeing the thoughts, impulses, and anger or fear he tries to keep supressed.

Though Palahniuk uses this narrative technique "to pique interest, create suspense, and convey his characters' misconceptions, which are not fully sorted out until the conclusions," it is hard to not also see this desire to suppress key information as a trauma response – a certain "survival mode" or instinct (Vickroy 156). Distrust, among other symptoms ("a split self, constricted emotion... altered perceptual, decisional, and relational processes..."), is a common trope in Palahniuk's protagonists and characters: an unwillingness to share pain with the world (Vickroy 164).

Singing for Silence: Lullabies, Culling Songs and Other Incantations

Much of this chapter, thus far, has dealt with trauma's role in the narrative of *Lullaby* – yet I have remained silent on the role of lullabies themselves. What is the shared thread between trauma and lullabies (either the fictional "culling song" vaguely described in *Lullaby* itself, or real lullabies in the world)?[4] The connection, on first glance, seems rather opaque.

What is the function of a lullaby? At its very core, though a singular definition of lullabies is difficult to parse, it is any song prescribed with the function of putting a child to sleep. In the dark of the home, in those most intimate spaces, the lullaby places one at rest in a world of thunderous noise.

In this section of the chapter, I explore various incantations found in cultures around the world, exploring various lullabies and spells intended to quiet the world. Lullabies, this section claims, are considered functional and magical responses to various traumas, recited to dispel various effects of said trauma and return the world (or more directly, the domestic) to a state of peace. Noise from the crib, or in the arms of a parent rocking a child gently to sleep, is often framed as a disruptive force on two levels: (1) on a basic level, within the domestic sphere, and (2) on a universal and magical level, an effort to make peace with various spirits disrupted by the cries from the cradle.

Lullabies, we should note, are not silent; however, they are often quietly sung in a soothing tone to the recipient. Songs designed to bring noise to an end, to bring peace to a chaotic crib. What use is noise to silence noise? Lullabies act as a form of reparative sound, working to restore a broken balance or trauma in the home or world, returning it to an idealized silence in need of healing. It is, if anything, a form of magical incantation and dialogue with metaphysical forces to ensure things are set right.

The song described in *Lullaby*, then, is described here as a transgressive extension of this magical logic. While lullabies seek to temporarily mend traumatic disturbances of noise in the world, Palahniuk's song is designed with the intention to cull or bring a permanent quiet to such noise and suffering from the invocation of death. Further, in the hands of the characters in the book, a song whose function is to relieve the suffering of loved ones becomes weaponized, used for all manner of sordid murders.

---

[4] The titular lullaby (or culling song) of *Lullaby* is never revealed to the reader throughout the novel, adding an air of mystery to the narrative. Though we, as readers, witness the unintentional consequences of Carl's memorization of the lullaby/culling song, we never even glimpse a single stanza of the song itself. However, what we do know is that the song is designed to provide a painless death to those who are aged, ill, or starving to death.

In "Magic at the Cradle: Babylonian and Assyrian Lullabies," Walter Faber explores evidence surrounding potential lullabies found in Ancient Mesopotamia where a lullaby or other folk-poetry acts as a "formula of magic power"—a part of a wider "magico-medical corpus" of incantations with the function of stilling the body and counteracting illnesses of various types.[5]

One such candidate for an Old Babylonian era lullaby Faber analyzes is rendered here:

> Little one, who dwelt in the house of darkness –
>
> well, you are outside now, have seen the light of the sun.
>
> Why are you crying? Why are you yelling?
>
> Why didn't you cry in there?
>
> You have roused the god of the house, the *kusarikkum*[6] has woken up:
>
> "Who roused me? Who startled me?"
>
> The little one has roused you, the little one has startled you!
>
> "As onto drinkers of wine, as onto tipplers,
>
> may sleep fall upon him!" (Faber 140)

The proposed lullaby's content is quite simply understood as the cries of the child (who once dwelt in the "house of darkness" – the womb) that have violently interrupted the domestic peace and woken both the god of the house and its protective spirits. What is required to return to said state of peace is "a short dialogue between the god of the house and the speaker" before the god uses magic to put the child to sleep (Faber, 141). A second Old Babylonian era candidate for a lullaby bears many similarities:

---

[5] Faber draws on Erica Reiner's (1985) inquiry into an Akkadian folk-poem about the 'Heart Grass' (*šammu ša libbi*) – a mythological plant whose medicinal properties are tied to the invocation of the sun deity, where the poem is meant to be read as an incantation/invocation of the god to intervene on behalf of the ill person, curing them of a wounded heart or other ailments of the body (*libbu*).

[6] The *kusarikkum* describe in this lullaby is, per Faber, a "benevolent protective spirit in the shape of a bison with a human head" tasked with the guarding of the house.

> You there, little one, newborn human being,
>
> you have indeed come out, have seen the sunlight.
>
> Why didn't you ever treat you mother like this in there?
>
> Instead of being nice to your father, letting your mother lead a normal life
>
> you have startled the nursemaid, have disturbed the wet nurse.
>
> Because of your crying the god of the house cannot sleep, the goddess of the house remains sleepless
>
> Whom should I send to *Enkidu*[7] who fixed the night watches as three in number [, telling him]:
>
> "Let the one who overcame the gazelle also overcome him,
>
> let the one who bound the gazelle's kid also bind him."
>
> May someone he meets give him his sleep in the back country,
>
> may an ox-driver let him have his sleep!
>
> Until his mother awakens him, may he not wake up! (Faber, 142-143)

Again, we see many similar motifs within these verses with those preceding it, making note of (1) the disturbance of both mortals and gods, and (2) the need for a lyrical dialogue with deities to provide an incantation for the child (and members of the house) to properly rest.

Within these ancient verses, which Faber considers prototypical lullabies, there is a clear problem: noise offends the natural order of the night. In a time where things ought to be silent, or at least quieted, the rousing cries of an infant have the capacity to upset the delicate nature of silence for gods and humans. As Bledar Kondi writes in the *SAGE International Encyclopedia of Music and Culture*, drawing on both Albanian and Ainu examples, lullabies

---

[7] The *Enkidu* spoken of in this verse is popularly known as the friend of the legendary Mesopotamian king Gilgamesh of Uruk, protagonist of the *Epic of Gilgamesh* (an ancient epic poem).

may "comprise some of the earliest ethical instructions for children," often imploring them to remember their duties towards both family and the larger world (Kondi 1356). For these ancient verses, the injunction seems clear: avoid the disturbance of the order of things.

Kondi also notes a congruity between lullabies and songs of lament and loss, suggesting that various local traditions "draw on the same stock of poetic and melodic formulas" in crafting them. There seems, on this account, to be a likeness between the silence of the cradle at rest and the grave, a quieting of pain and suffering. Kondi writes that a "lullaby song when a child dies portrays the universal images of death as sleep, whereas the lament sung to put the child to sleep airs misfortunes of every kind." Consider the following "lullaby of death" Kondi draws from traditions of the Gulf of Finland:

> I'm rocking my baby under the turf...
>
> Come Death along the marsh... [...]
>
> Would that Death... take our apple away...
>
> I would make socks for Death... (Nenola-Kallio, 106-107)

One could almost imagine the culling song of *Lullaby* resembling such a lullaby: a poetic incantation invoking the spirit of Death to take away the suffering of a child and bringing it the sleep of the grave. Here, rather than rocking a child in the cradle, the child is quite literally rocked into the earth, with a lyrical dialogue (not unlike the preceding Babylonian examples) with Death to carry the child into silence. Though no audible disturbance has broken the balance of silence, silence here is articulated as a space where no suffering may take place.

Thus, lullabies are understood to serve a particular magical function: the silencing of traumatic noise. The song itself acts as a reparative force to heal the environment of the home or of losing one's loved ones. Suffering is purged. Here, however, students might rightly ask, can the same be said for Carl at the end of *Lullaby*? Good pedagogy would press them to consider how the unresolved ending of *Lullaby* might lead to several potential answers, or even speculative writing assignments aimed to re-work the ending of the novel itself. Perhaps, in a more intriguing manner, students might even craft their own version of the culling song, reacting to the examples offered within this chapter.

Seeking Silence: Conclusions

What should be the takeaway of this chapter, winding through gothic horror, trauma theory, and lullabies across the world? If teachers can guide students in paying close attention to the multi-faceted cultural roots of Palahniuk's work—rather than merely focus on transgressive social criticism, both will come away with some useful insights for how one might read *Lullaby* (and, perhaps, Palahniuk's wider corpus).

An opportunity for students to see the limitations of a singular critical approach can be addressed in the way simply adhering to a social critique reading of Palahniuk's work is, while certainly acceptable, liable to miss the importance of noise and silence within the novel. Rather than merely a matter of media mind pollution (or control), noise comes to represent a traumatic force in this chapter. Noise illustrates how trauma not only affects individuals like Carl who suffer from conditions like PTSD and hyperacusis, but also how one's ability to tell their story because of trauma can be complicated by the noise of their condition and life. Silence, on the other hand, is not necessarily seen (as Helen, Oyster and Carl's words in *Lullaby* suggest) to be a form of control and domination. Rather, silence is seen as a reaction to said traumatic noise, a desire to create a safe and reparative space in a world that is fragmented and inhospitable.

But does Carl ever get the silence he has been longing for? Like many of Palahniuk's works, the ending of the work leaves one to speculate. It is worth noting, according to Vickroy:

> Palahniuk complicates healing from trauma, particularly for men, because clinically speaking, healing necessitates acknowledging helplessness, which contradicts the masculine identity formed in bodies acting out. (159)

Carl, like many of Palahniuk's male characters, refuses to confront his trauma directly until the end of the book, using a coping strategy of smashing models beneath his feet or violently lashing out with the culling song at various characters in the book. It isn't really until his killing of Nash and reunion with Helen (albeit in another form) that Carl finally utters the names of his wife and daughter in a frank manner – confronting his traumatic past.

Further, in uttering the phrases "We're all of us haunted and haunting," Carl finally admits that he is indeed haunted by trauma in his life, and that he has not been in control of his life (Palahniuk 258). Returning to the theme of the Gothic loop, the goal (on this account) is to finally reach a point where one can re-start with a better position. Carl may not yet have achieved the silence and safety which he craves, but by recognizing his traumatic position, he might yet have a chance at healing.

Works Cited

Baguley, David M. "Hyperacusis." *Journal of the Royal Society of Medicine*, vol. 96, no. 12, Dec. 2003, pp. 582–585.

Collado-Rodríguez, Francisco. "Textual Unreliability, Trauma, and The Fantastic in Chuck Palahniuk's *Lullaby.*'" *Studies in the Novel*, vol. 45, no. 4, University of North Texas, 2013, pp. 620–637.

Faber, Walter. "Magic at the Cradle: Babylonian and Assyrian Lullabies," *Anthropos*, vol. 85, 1990, pp. 139-148.

Green, John. "Palahniuk, Chuck. Lullaby." *Booklist*, vol. 98, no. 22, Aug. 2002, pp. 1887.

Juranovszky, Andrea. "Trauma Re-enactment in the Gothic Loop: A Study on Structures of Circularity in Gothic Fiction". *Inquiries Journal/Student Pulse*, vol. 6, no. 05, 2014.

Keesey, Douglas. *Understanding Chuck Palahniuk*. U of SC P, 2016.

Kondi, Bledar. "Lullabies." In *The SAGE International Encyclopedia of Music and Culture*, edited by Janet Sturman, 1355-56. SAGE Publications, 2019.

Mendieta, Eduardo. "Surviving American Culture: On Chuck Palahniuk." *Philosophy and Literature*, vol. 29, no. 2, 2005, pp. 394–408.

McCracken, David. *Chuck Palahniuk and the Comic Grotesque: Subversion of Ideology in the Fiction*. McFarland & Co., 2020.

Morton, K. Willis. "Lullaby at the Fight Club: The Chuck Palahniuk Gob Q & A." *Gobshite Quarterly*, Feb. 2003, www.gobshitequarterly.com/arkive/issue001/morton_lullaby_gobqa_eng.htm.

Nenola-Kallio, Aili. *Studies in Ingrian Laments*. FFC, 1982.

Palahniuk, Chuck. *Lullaby: A Novel*. Anchor Books, 2003.

Palumbo, Devon B., et al. "Misophonia and potential underlying mechanisms: a perspective." *Frontiers in Psychology*, vol. 9, 2018, pp. 1-8.

Stevens, Kevin. "'Eccentric Murmurs': Noise, Voice, and Unreliable Narration in Jane Eyre." *Narrative (Columbus, Ohio)*, vol. 26, no. 2, 2018, pp. 201–220.

Rouw, Romke, and Mercede Erfanian. "A large-scale study of misophonia." *Journal of Clinical Psychology*, vol. 74, no. 3, 2018, pp. 453-479.

Vickroy, Laurie. *Reading Trauma Narratives: The Contemporary Novel and the Psychology of Oppression*. University of VA P, 2015.

Zeigler, Robert. "Having the last word: Chuck Palahniuk's Lullaby." *Notes on Contemporary Literature*, vol. 37, no. 4, 2007, p. 4.

Chapter 6

Gut-Check: The Risks of Defining and Re-Defining Capital "L" Literature as an Adjunct

Christopher Burlingame

Mount Aloysius College

Abstract: While I've never been one to play it as safe as sticking to publisher's anthology when putting together a reading list for courses like Rhetoric II: An Introduction to Literature or Creative Writing, prepping Chuck Palahniuk's "Guts" for a class at the small, Catholic liberal arts college where I work as a professional writing tutor and adjunct, left me feeling like a had decision to make that equalled the predicament facing the story's narrator. I included "Guts" on my syllabus, in part, because of the lore around people passing out and throwing up at public readings, but it had been nearly ten years since I'd read the story for myself. I always re-read what I'm teaching the day I teach it, and I found myself in a panic over the graphic and cavalier descriptions of masturbation and self-mutilation. I vaguely remembered finding Palahniuk's inclusion of these details titillating as a younger reader, but they left me fearing for my job. I fired off an email warning to students and sweated it out until my class later that evening. In class, I didn't have to give my students the option to discuss "Guts" or simply move on to one of our other readings. They were already abuzz about it when I walked in. It was one of the most productive class discussions I'd ever had about craft in a creative writing class, so much so that I included it on my syllabus the next semester for Honors Rhetoric II. The reality remains, all that had to happen was to have one student complain to administration, and the president of our college could have dispensed with the tenuous position I hold. I still feel like I'm constantly looking to the surface and having to decide to bite the guts floating in front of me or drown.

Keywords: Chuck Palahniuk, "Guts," Creative Writing, Adjuncts

***

I was going to throw up.

I was going to pass out.

And I hadn't even gotten to the part of the story that gave it its name.

My hands shook, rattling a version of Chuck Palahniuk's "Guts'' that I'd printed out from his fansite, chuckpalahniuk.net.

Before the semester started, I had included the story on the syllabus precisely for the mythos surrounding the way it had provoked physical reactions from audiences at public readings (Keesey 61; McCracken 14). If it made audience members at Palahniuk's public readings faint, it would be a great example to share with young creative writers who were learning about the power of words. According to McCracken, "[u]nequivocally, the visceral 'effect' of Palahniuk's transgressive descriptions is a defining quality of his literary expertise" (14).

But there was a problem.

It had been more than ten years since I'd read the story in *Haunted*. I possessed only the vaguest memory that it was shocking and disturbing—something I remembered loving, but time had rounded the story's sharp edges for me. For the first time in more than seven years of teaching on the college level, I realized I may have gone too far.

I was going to get fired.

***

I had about an hour before my first scheduled tutoring appointment. I started some coffee in the library's back office and wove through the first floor, past wooden tables and chairs and computer stations, to my desk in the Learning Commons to mark up my readings for my creative writing class that night. I work as a professional writing tutor during the day, and each semester, I pick up a few evening classes. I have a single-credit teaching requirement in my contract, but to paraphrase David Gooblar's introduction to *The Missing Course*, "Teaching wasn't just an annoying requirement" of my position, "it was a calling" I devoted myself to developing "as an adjunct with little to no institutional support and few colleagues to talk to" (5). While freshman composition or a developmental writing course were the most commonly assigned classes because of how they fit with my role as academic support staff, being the only person on campus with an MFA in creative writing meant that, every other year, I got to teach our 300-level creative writing course. It became my baby. It was the thing that kept me motivated even when I felt like I was getting buried under nearly 1,000 individual tutoring sessions in one semester.

With little oversight beyond submitting my syllabus for the department secretary to have on file, I had the freedom to rebuild the course from scratch each time I taught it. I called it "taking the course down to the studs," a process that I found to be almost as exhilarating as actually teaching. I treated this class as an opportunity to experiment, push boundaries and grow as a teacher, and *I hate doing the same thing twice*. Also, because there is no prerequisite requirement for the course, and students could take it more than once, I had to change the focus and subtitle each time I taught it. Beyond all that, I get bored easily. I really identify with David Gooblar's claim that "[s]tudents are my discipline, and every semester they change and I have to try to become proficient in that discipline all over again" (8). So, with each iteration, and in the pursuit of good teaching—"the practice of helping others learn"—I strayed further and further from conventional, anthologized works that had been used in my own education as a fiction writer (Gooblar 8). Alongside fiction, poetry, drama, and essays that could be found in literary journals or edited collections, I taught snippets of transgressive fiction, music and film, graphic novels, stories told in Tweets, and video games.

The first time I ever taught the course, my "edgy" pieces were Tom Perrotta's novel, *Little Children*, and a creative nonfiction piece, "Bare," one of my MFA classmates, Caroline Horwitz, published about her experience with boudoir photography. I thought these pieces' descriptions of sexuality made them risque for teaching at a private catholic institution, but I grew to appreciate that my students' thresholds were often greater than I gave them credit for. With that said, in the back of my mind, I knew it only took one student complaining to administration for my position to be endangered or even eliminated. I used to joke with my students and co-workers, "I hope I don't get fired for this," or "If I'm not here tomorrow, someone complained to the administration," on nights when I had something planned that I thought was a little beyond the pale. These statements may seem ridiculous to those advocates of academic freedom, especially those protected by tenure. Unfortunately, the reality for those of us working as adjuncts, especially those at small colleges like mine, who signed an initial contract with vaguely threatening language about "serving at the pleasure of the President," is that we lead more precarious existences that consciously and subconsciously factor into what we feel comfortable teaching.

Some jokes are funny until they're not.

Getting Up the "Guts" to Use Palahniuk in Creative Writing

Some of the previous subtitles for my creative writing course included Contemporary Storytelling, Narrative Frontiers, and Re-Writing What Literature Can Be, but in the Fall of 2019, the focus was Writing for Popular Audiences. I know this sounds like an odd course subtitle under which to find work by Palahniuk, who is so classified, often with the intent of dismissing his work as sub-literary, as transgressive; however, his work is regularly on bestseller lists, and "he is an author with a cult following, [and] that cult is large" (Keesey 3). In *Transgressive Fiction: The New Satiric Tradition*, Robin Mookerjee refers to how, in 1993 while writing for the *Los Angeles Times*, Michael Silverblatt "characterized transgressive novelists as those who deliberately include unpleasant content - taboo sex, violence, and drug use - solely to provoke the reader" (1). While Silverblatt's definition is a commonly cited reference point, I find it to be a bit reductive to say the inclusion of any content—good, bad or otherwise—has any singular purpose. A primary focus of my pedagogy in the Writing for Popular Audiences run for creative writing was trying to bring my student to understanding that labels, like transgressive, genre, or horror, even if they seem to work to the advantage of an author or piece of work, may be unnecessarily restrictive. For example, Stephen King writes horror, but he should be considered much more than a horror writer, and Jenji Kohan, writer and creator of *Weeds* and *Orange is the New Black*, writes comedy, but her work is much more emotionally complex than getting to a punch line.

With this iteration of the course, I was aware that I had some students on my roster who had taken my Narrative Frontiers version of the course. Since that edition of the class focused on breaking forms and re-conceiving ways of producing literature, I wanted to gear this class toward considering genres and types of stories that sold well and address the commercial side of producing art. My decision to take this route was to show students that works resonate with audiences and succeed commercially because of the same characteristics that make "L"iterature *serious* art and worthy of academic study. I wanted students to be able to recognize that there are any number of categories and genres of creative expression that regularly find audiences, and make a profit, as a way to dispel the myth of the 'real' artist toiling in obscurity and poverty only to later be championed by critics and scholars. I wanted students to get inside these commercially successful works and understand what makes each tick so they could experiment with the respective genres in weekly writing assignments that received online commentary from their classmates and myself. We also conducted bi-weekly workshops that ranged from one-on-one interactions to small groups to speed dating to the full class offering input on these experiments. By providing students with constantly changing genres of readings that can be validated as engaging due to their bestselling statuses, I hoped to overcome the "number of studies that have consistently demonstrated that the majority of college students—perhaps as many as 80 percent—regularly come to class not having done the reading" and eliminate the implicit snobbery of getting stuck in the canon of short stories, poems, and novels that are regularly taught in entry-entry level creative writing courses (Gooblar 83). Don't get me wrong, I love O'Connor, Oates, Hemingway, and all the others, but especially among my students, who are mostly not English majors, I think it's important for them to, first, enjoy what they're reading and to see it as attainable, accessible, and a part of the popular culture with which they are constantly engaging and contributing to already.

So, prior to getting to "Guts," we spent weeks discussing college-age writing prodigies like Bret Easton Ellis and J.D. Salinger with samples from Marina Keegan's *The Opposite of Loneliness*. This grouping was selected to show them that writing doesn't have to be something you're good at when you're older. Next, we examined minimalism by reading chapter six of *Fight Club*. In previous versions of my creative writing classes, I had often referenced *Fight Club* while teaching variations on narrative structure, but I had always resisted teaching it in creative writing, afraid it might get spoiled for me. However, I felt freed up to include it and some more of Palahniuk's work in this go-around with the creative writing class due to the success I found the year before with the man-i-verse and teaching research writing in Rhetoric II (which is documented in the earlier chapter in this collection). Beyond that, my previous students' most consistent critique in creative writing was that they wished I'd added *Fight Club* to the reading list so they could understand just what the hell I was going on about, causing the comments in my IDEA course evaluations to include statements like "Make Fight Club part of the course :) [sic]" and "a prerequisite should be reading Fight Club [sic]." In addition to chapter six of *Fight Club*, and to round out our discussion of minimalism, we read works about and by a major stylistic influence on Palahniuk, Amy Hempel. That discussion was lively, especially among the students who had already taken my Narrative Frontiers creative writing class and had pushed me to include something from *Fight Club*. The whole class also produced really impressive writing about secrets that corresponded with Hempel's "The Cemetery Where Al Jolson is Buried" and were informed by Palahniuk's essay "Not Chasing Amy" from *Stranger than Fiction*.

We spent other weeks talking about the marketability of dystopias with *The Handmaid's Tale* graphic novel and the pilot episode of the Hulu series. We delved into how works can be translated with "What We Lost in the Fire." We studied thrillers and the scandals around them with A.J. Finn's *The Woman in the Window* because there was an exposé on the author that appeared in *The New Yorker* and a film that was supposed to be released the same week we were reading it but got pushed back to 2021. This was an experiment of including work on the syllabus where we could go to the movie theater (when that was still a thing), as a class, to watch and discuss a mainstream adaptation that ultimately did not come to fruition. We did look at some canon short story stalwarts of capital "L" literature from *The New Yorker* like Ann Beattie, Raymond Carver and Alice Munro by juxtaposing them with relative newcomers like Junot Diaz, Jennifer Egan, and Z.Z. Packer. Later, we'd look at franchises like *Harry Potter* and *The Hunger Games* and Young Adult literature like John Green's *The Fault in Our Stars* and Jason Reynolds' *Long Way Down* that were adapted to film or slated to be. Among all of that, in the fall of 2019, during the first class after Halloween, we were getting to our unit in horror, and we were reading "Guts."

That Fateful Day

Spoiler alert!: I would, on that day and others, teach "Guts."

Before I go any further though, for the uninitiated, "Guts" is a story about masturbation that leads to mutilation, and how a "chronic sense of shame" can lead the self-pleasuring party to have to choose between life and death (Palahniuk, "Guts"). It appeared in the March 2004 issue of *Playboy* before becoming a part of Palahniuk's novel-in-stories horror homage to *The Canterbury Tales* and *The Decameron*, 2005's *Haunted*. The story begins as a conversational relaying of urban legend meets "this-guy-I-know" stories about masturbation "gone wrong. Horribly wrong" and needing medical intervention or families covering up death by autoerotique asphyxiation. The story escalates to a first-person account of a character who engages in "Pearl Diving" or "whacking off underwater" at the deep end of the pool while sitting naked on "the inlet port for the swimming pool filter and the circulation pump" and then collecting the "big, fat, milky gobs" of semen that were left floating through the water after he had finished (Palahniuk, "Guts"). *I know. I know what you're thinking—how could I have thought this was a good idea?*

But wait! It gets worse.

One day, while pearl diving, the unnamed narrator finishes and pushes off the bottom of the pool to return to the surface to get some air before collecting his semen, and he feels a pull, saying, "My ass is stuck" (Palahniuk,

"Guts"). When he persists in pushing off the bottom of the pool, his rectum prolapses, and his intestines get sucked out of him by the filter. At first unaware of why he can't make it to the surface, he says "I turn and look back...but it doesn't make sense. This thick rope, some kind of snake, blue-white braided with veins has come up out of the pool drain and it's holding on to my butt" (Palahniuk, "Guts"). And this next detail is what Keesey writes that Palahniuk acknowledges "'made seated people go limp' and faint to the floor": "The stuff you're digesting, doctor's call it fecal matter. Higher up is chyme, pockets of thin runny mess studded with *corn and peanuts* and round green peas" (62; Palahniuk, emphasis mine). His first thought is about getting his swimsuit back on because "God forbid my folks see my dick" (Palahniuk, "Guts"). The dilemma of the story, the real life and death choice the narrator must make, is to either drown and be caught in the compromising position of having died while masturbating or survive and suffer the medical implications, and potential death, from biting through his own intestines and pulling himself from the water. Palahniuk switches to second-person to draw the reader into the experience with lines like "You let go for second, and you're gutted...You swim for the surface, for a breath, and you're gutted...You don't swim, and you drown" (Palahniuk, "Guts"). The narrator acknowledges, "It's hard to say what my parents were more disgusted by: how I got in trouble or how I'd saved myself" (Palahniuk, "Guts").

For those of you reading and wondering just "what-the-actual-fuck" I was thinking, before I tell you: *that's not all*, let me pause to apologize to my mom and my wife, both public school educators and neither of whom know that I taught and continue to teach this story. *Sorry, not sorry*—until I am.

I'm sure my time is coming. They know I teach and write about transgressive literature but would probably blanch at reading or talking about the things that feel a little too commonplace to me. They have both asked me why I don't write happy stories when I write fiction. And, they are both rightfully worried about how I shouldn't be doing anything to intentionally endanger my tenuous position as an adjunct, but more on that later.

Although I've spoiled the climax of the story, I think it's best for the curious reader to have some surprises left in Palahniuk's resolution and get to my own moments in the classroom with "Guts." Despite Palahniuk's narrator saying, "Now you can take a good deep breath," deep breaths were in short supply for me in November 2019. As I panicked and let my coffee burn in the back room, I fired off the following Announcement in Canvas, our college's learning management system, which also got sent to all my students' email accounts:

Subject: I'm feeling a little "guts"-less

Okay,

So, I have to admit that I've lost my nerve a little bit for my first time as a teacher.

I have been re-reading Chuck Palahniuk's "Guts," and I'm worried it might be a bit MUCH, so I am going to make it an **optional** reading.

Tonight, as a class, we can decide if we want to discuss it or let it go.

It is far more sexually explicit than I recall (it's been about 10 years since I last read it), but I initially wanted to read it because of the people passing out and throwing up when Palahniuk included it at his public readings. This kind of provocative stuff has always interested me, but time away from this story has caused the severity of it to soften in my memory.

Now, I am a little worried that this may be putting too many of you in a really uncomfortable position. In some ways, I wanted to teach it to look at how extreme horror can be, but I am questioning my own judgment.

The ball is in your court. We'll still have plenty to discuss, even without the Palahniuk piece.

CB

It is obviously not my finest composition or my most confident moment in education, but my rapport with the students, in part as the professional writing tutor and with this class in particular, was such that this level of raw honesty felt necessary and appropriate.

I can't say at what line in the story the panic first set in, but it was somewhere between the lines about a carrot where, "He slathers it with grease and grinds his ass down on it...Nothing happens except it hurts" and one about candle wax where "Stoned and horny, he slips it down inside, deeper and deeper into the piss slit of his boner" (Palahniuk, "Guts"). I often tell students that despite my fair complexion making my face prone to flushing red, there is very little that embarrasses me, truly embarrasses me. Even now, I wasn't embarrassed for myself in assigning this piece as much as I was worried about the position I felt I had placed the students. I always want my students to feel like no topic should be off the table for discussion or for becoming the subject of their own writing, so I make sure to slip a "fuck" into conversation on the first night of class and regularly share personal experiences like getting lost in Amsterdam's red-light district with just a rubber duckie-patterned umbrella as my only defense after witnessing a man being thrown in a canal for taking pictures or about having to read aloud a piece of fiction I had written about an explicit glory hole experience during my first workshop with two-time Queen's medal winner, Don Paterson, at the University of St. Andrews in Scotland. Keesey cites Palahniuk as saying, "'My way of handling unpleasant things is to reframe the painful and uncomfortable things and turn them into stories and make them funny. The act of writing is a way of tricking yourself into revealing something that you would never consciously put into the world" (109). But, with my students, especially because most of them are uninitiated in the vulnerable act of sharing their work, I always offer to read the work aloud if they are uncomfortable doing so. I recognize that most of my students are not seasoned creative writers with a wealth of workshop experience and the necessary thick skin for receiving and growing from critiques of emotionally raw writing. For most of them, my creative writing class, at least initially, seemed like an easy upper-level English course, but many of them quickly adapt into perceiving themselves as and becoming serious writers. Even still, asking my Saudi students to comment on a line like "those Arab guys are pretty damn smart. They've totally re-invented jacking off" or asking my predominately female class to talk about male masturbation in such explicit detail seems like a big ask (Palahniuk, "Guts").

***

I finished eating my dinner in the staff break room right next to my classroom, tucked my chin into my chest and entered the class not knowing what to say, where to start or where to look first, but what I had not accounted for was something that I had fostered unconsciously throughout the semester that was going to turn my day around: my students had become a community with shared values. In *Distracted: Why Students Can't Focus and What You Can Do About It*, James Lang notes that teachers can hold student attention by taking the "initial step to build community in the classroom" and "help them feel secure in their seats," but I had not done this explicitly by directly surveying students or anything like that. Instead, my students seemed to have arrived at shared values of openness and graciousness with handling difficult or challenging subject matter organically through our interactions in the weeks leading up to this one, and not only were we going to talk about "Guts" that night, they wanted to dive right in.

I flipped on an extra row of fluorescents and looked up for the first time to a raised hand. The student was one who had taken an earlier version of this class. She was also a work study in the library who had been coming to tutoring sessions with drafts of her creative work since the last time I'd taught creative writing. She said, "We want to start with 'Guts.'"

"Are you sure?" I asked, trying to make eye contact with all of the students in the seats they had arranged in the back of the classroom.

Another hand, another voice, "I didn't know why we were reading this with horror, but I think it has something to do with this weird intersection of the thing we aren't supposed to talk about and that thing becoming real. What did you all think about the parents trying to make the teen suicide 'better' on the second page?"

I wheeled the whiteboard over and started taking notes for them. As Palahniuk's narrator says, "So listen as fast as you can."

Papers rustled, but they were already on the same page.

The Guts of Teaching "Guts"

So, what did we talk about? What did we do with the story after the first student directed the class to talk about covering up sexually-associated teen suicides? This is the premise of the 2009 Robin Williams film, *World's Greatest Dad*. It might be a good pair for a lesson on "Guts." First, we handled the beginning of that paragraph which states, "Looking back, kid-psych experts, school counselors now say that the last peak in teen suicides was kids trying to choke while they beat off" (Palahniuk, "Guts"). This paragraph, like so many found in Palahniuk's work, reveals a clever device that is essential to creating the suspension of disbelief by dropping details that are or sound like facts or are at least plausible enough to lend credibility to the narrator. This device is seemingly omnipresent in Palahniuk's work from the instructions for making explosives in *Fight Club* to the code words for danger in *Choke* to porn history in *Snuff* to Hollywood trivia in *Tell-All*, and so on. With each new work, Palahniuk seems to deploy a new set of facts to construct a reality in which, despite whatever otherwise absurdist elements may appear, the story will still feel passable to most readers.

During our discussion of this technique and how students could imitate in their work, one of the students pulled up "Not Chasing Amy," an essay we had used to discuss minimalism in the second week of class, and pointed to a passage that had Palahniuk describing Amy Hempel's fiction as "so tight, so boiled down to facts, that all you can do is lie on the floor, face down, and praise it" (145). The students said that these facts could be a part of world-building, especially if the horror fiction they were writing was set in a slightly alternate reality. Students said any changes to the rules that govern our reality could create a disconcerting and eerie feeling. One student pointed to our work with *The Handmaid's Tale* and the relaying of facts unique to Gilead while another went back to "Guts" to point out the "Spirit on the Stairway" reference point about the French having a term for a common phenomenon that must be translated and its variations for the way it becomes a "horse" in the story (Palahniuk, "Guts;" "Not Chasing Amy" 143). In "Not Chasing Amy," Palahniuk describes a horse as a theme or chorus, and explains it is one of the four main elements of minimalism Palahniuk learned in Tom Spanbauer's workshop. Palahniuk says, "[i]n minimalism, a story is a symphony, building and building, but never losing the original melody line" (Palahniuk, "Not Chasing Amy" 143). I pointed students to the lines in "Guts" like "Not even French people talk about EVERYTHING" after giving the fact "Emergency paramedics will tell you every year about 150 people get stuck this way, sucked by a circulation pump. Get your long hair caught, or your ass, and you're going to drown. Every year, tons of people do. Most of them in Florida." We talked about how these variations tie back to the Spirit on the Stairway concept and how it becomes a transitional device that continues to evolve to a Russian phrase being translated to ultimately the narrator adopting it himself in response to "[a]ll those people grossed out or feeling sorry for me...I need that like I need teeth in my asshole" (Palahniuk, "Guts").

Although I love "Not Chasing Amy," I had not considered pairing it with "Guts." For me, the essay was much more about Hempel, and on the few other occasions I'd taught it, it was in conjunction with Hempel's story, "The Harvest," so this was an impromptu connection made by my students. The thing that had made Palahniuk's audiences pass out and that had made me so anxious as a teacher, even though it's the reason I wanted to teach "Guts," can be found in Palahniuk's very brief discussion of "[w]hat Tom Spanbauer and Gordon Lish call 'going on the body', [*sic*] to give the reader a sympathetic physical reaction, to involve the reader on a gut level" ("Not Chasing Amy" 145). This can be seen in the on-the-bodiness of a line like "If I told you how it tasted, you would never, ever again eat calamari" because it is physically revolting and retch-inducing after saying "You bite and snap at your own ass. You run out of air, and you will chew through anything to get that next breath" (Palahniuk, "Guts"). We talked about how lines like this, where the focus is on both a familiarity with and a mutilation of the body *as it is supposed to be*, is also essential to the thrills one finds in physical horror like Regan's body contorted and spewing vomit in *The Exorcist* or the potential of one of Jigsaw's devices destroying a body in the *Saw* franchise.

One more key element to talk about in the context of the creative writing classroom that my students felt compelled to discuss was the way humor was used to make the violence to the body, and horror of it all, more tolerable. They wanted to talk about how the humor was both related to the bodily discomfort they felt while also diverting their attention away from it and defusing its impact enough to enable them to keep reading. A line that they really found funny, but not ha-ha funny, dealt with how "some deeds" that are "even too low to get talked about" can have long-term consequences on a person's life trajectory. For the boy with the wax in his penis, his parents "paid for the bladder operation with his college fund. One stupid mistake, and now he'll never be a lawyer" (Palahniuk, "Guts"). The students like how the humor requires them to connect some of the dots themselves and how this becomes another kind of horse when the narrator says, "I never got a football scholarship. Never got an MBA" (Palahniuk, "Guts"). This is linking the wax-in-the-penis friend with the narrator's father having him take a vitamin to play football, even though he skipped practice to masturbate in the pool, with the "pool guy" fishing "out a rubbery tube, a watery hank of intestine with a big orange vitamin pill still inside" (Palahniuk, "Guts"). For my students, they likened this tying together of threads to some of their favorite stand-up comedians having several smaller punch lines accumulate to the larger pay-off that they use to end their set. What my students took away from reading and discussing this story was very structural, but it was not necessarily the way I expected it to work out.

We had other stories on the agenda that night, but I couldn't get them to stop talking about "Guts."

Covering Your Ass: Justifying Ditching the Canon

It is no secret to me that my privilege in teaching evening classes like creative writing makes me part of what Dan Clawson and Max Page describe in 2011's *The Future of Higher Education* as the "move to a more disposable faculty" as being "very much a part of the university-as-business model" (43). In this model, I am afforded very few protections and lack even the most basic security of knowing what, when, or if I will be teaching next, but I do not say this to complain. I know that my full-time staff position makes me more financially stable than most working in this adjunctified reality. While I mentioned before that my wife would be upset with the financial impact of my losing these teaching opportunities, her bigger concern is always the way my decisions in the classroom, from the language I employ to the works I select to the types of assignments I challenge students to complete, all have the potential to endanger my staff position, especially at a Catholic institution. I have stopped telling her what I teach or say in my classes because part of me must live in denial of her awareness of the precariousness of my position in order for me to be able to use the material to its fullest potential for inspiring engagement, conversation and lasting learning that is more than the "simple process of remembering ideas and information" (Bain 17). I am most myself in the "natural critical learning environment" of my classroom and interacting with students as the proverbial lightbulb flickers to life in the wake of reading "stories that will 'grab them by the throat'" (Bain 17; McCracken 15). But, my decision to include these works, like Palahniuk's "Guts," in my syllabi is a constant risk-reward scenario because, at any moment, one student complaint or one attentive department chair or administrator could bring it all crashing down, but it could also lead to a lasting learning opportunity that students are not soon to forget.

What I want to address is the way that adjunctification has the potential to inhibit learning by making teaching and content stale due to the perception that our contingent position means we should play it safe. At my institution, as I understand it is common in higher education, anthologies abound but I can't abide, and students responded positively in the IDEA course evaluations by writing "I never liked writing or reading in high school. I was always given books that didn't hold my interest. But this course allowed me to really expand my knowledge and show that not all books you read in class are boring." Another student noted, "This is my second time taking this course. I love writing and Chris has really helped me hone in my skills. I love this course...I know I would learn something new each time because the subject matter is not stagnant...If I could keep coming back just to take [h]is courses, I would." These comments indicate the value of what I'm doing in my creative writing classes by including *risky* works like "Guts," but as I said before I know my ability to take this risk is partly due to having a full-time staff position and partly to my own lack of common sense or sense of self-preservation. Even in my own education as a creative writer and student of literature, it was not really until my doctoral program that I found classes that departed much from the canon. While at the Indiana University of Pennsylvania, I took classes on the Black Arts Movement, video games, graphic novels, and created an independent study on transgressive fiction and adaptation, but too often, the classes that deaden student motivation to engage and learn can be a direct result of the tendency to play it safe. According to Rebecca Recco, writing for *EdSurge*:

> But in this day in age, when even the most high-ranking officials are saying and doing inappropriate things in the public eye, when our nation is starkly divided and intolerance creates a constant "us-versus-them" attitude among social groups, now is exactly the time to teach students how to deal with controversial subjects and how to cope with a plurality of ideas and identities.

It is for this reason that I think we have an obligation to teach works like "Guts." While "Guts" was a lens through which my creative writing students could understand story structure and how minimalist techniques like horses, burnt tongues, recording angels and going on the body can be translated to create effective horror, in my Honors Rhetoric II (our introduction to literature class), I use "Guts" to discuss how literature and more specifically, Palahniuk can take "advantage of the comic grotesque to warn readers against the exploitation of dominant ideologies" (McCracken 15). I wish that I had had access to critical texts like McCracken's *Chuck Palahniuk and the Comic Grotesque* or Keesey's *Understanding Chuck Palahniuk* that day in November. I would have felt that I had a better foundation from which to defend or justify my inclusion of this story, but I know this isn't something about which tenured faculty have to worry.

In my second year of helming the honors section of Rhetoric II, my students came to life in addressing the way in which so much of the injury and potential for death could be avoided by normalizing discussions of sexuality, sexual pleasure and kink. At the heart of "Guts" is the idea that we should hide what makes us feel good, and the danger comes in the concealment of that pleasure. From behind their masks in the spring of 2021, my honors students traced ways that other norms about race, gender, intelligence, and wealth have resulted in some form of marginalization or social injury. While the context of this class is different from my creative writing class, it was my panic that inspired the way I have found success in opening the discussion. With the floodgates to their reactions opening, my job is to get out of the way so my students can discover and dissect the story, as well as their own experiences, with one simple activity and a one-word question.

Before we dig in, I ask my students to look through "Guts" with a pen and draw a line where they had to stop reading. I follow-up with my single-word question: why?

While they explain what made them most uncomfortable and from where that discomfort is derived, the students entered discussions about our lines and limits. I share with them my experience of teaching this story in my creative writing class in 2019 and where I drew my own lines. I expose my own vulnerability and insecurity to free them up to share their own. The students talk about what it means to be offended. They talk about why being offended isn't necessarily a bad thing, but how more people could be better served by understanding that offense and how offense, as a response to something that is shocking, is a strategy that has been used by those in power to distract from a potentially greater issue of inequality or marginalization.

I may still get fired. That reality is always lurking, but I'm not going to stop teaching "Guts." I'm not flushed. I'm not embarrassed to teach this story or any others anymore because "[i]n the end, it's never what you worry about that gets you" (Palahniuk, "Guts"). If anything, I am embarrassed by my response and how little faith I had in my students' ability to be motivated to learn from this piece and how I almost deprived them of that opportunity.

At "Guts"'s narrator's behest, I can "take a good, deep breath," because when it comes to being afraid of teaching something, "I need that like I need teeth in my asshole."

Works Cited

Bain, Ken. *Super Courses: The Future of Teaching and Learning.* Princeton UP, 2021.

Clawson, Dan and Max Page. *The Future of Higher Education.* Routledge, 2011.

Gooblar, David. *The Missing Course: Everything They Never Taught You About College Teaching.* Harvard UP, 2019.

Keesey, Douglas. *Understanding Chuck Palahniuk.* The U of South Carolina P, 2016.

Lang, James M. *Distracted: Why Students Can't Focus and What You Can Do About It.* Basic, 2020.

McCracken, David. *Chuck Palahniuk and the Comic Grotesque: Subversion of Ideology in the Fiction.* McFarland & Co, 2020.

Mookerjee, Robin. *Transgressive Fiction: The New Satiric Tradition.* Palgrave MacMillan, 2013.

Palahniuk, Chuck. *Choke.* Anchor, 2002.

—. *Fight Club.* Anchor, 2005.

—. "Guts." *Chuck Palahniuk,* https://chuckpalahniuk.net/shorts/guts.

—. "Not Chasing Amy." *Stranger Than Fiction: True Stories.* Doubleday, 2004.

—. *Snuff.* Doubleday, 2008.

—. *Tell-All.* Anchor, 2011.

Recco, Rebecca. "Why We Need Controversies in Our Classrooms." *EdSurge,* 17 Jan. 2018, https://www.edsurge.com/news/2018-01-17-why-we-need-controversy-in-our-classrooms.

Chapter 7

Cassie Wright, Stormy Daniels, and #MeToo: Teaching Chuck Palahniuk's *Snuff* as a Response to Heteropatriarchy

David McCracken

Coker University

Abstract: Of all Palahniuk's novels, *Snuff* might be the one least likely taught in collegiate classes. Besides expecting questions after students discover the book is about a 600-man gangbang, instructors should anticipate inquiries from administrators concerning the rationale for selecting a porn star's swan song (one full of sexual references). Teaching *Snuff* is indeed a "gutsy" enterprise, but one worth pursuing if couched within the context of Stormy Daniel's (Stephanie Clifford's) private relationship with President Donald Trump and the proliferation of the #MeToo movement in American culture. The truth is that these are much more about power than sex, and sex is merely a vehicle through which power is asserted and manipulated. In *Anticlimax: A Feminist Perspective on the Sexual Revolution*, Sheila Jeffreys calls for a rethinking of heterosexuality in terms of its reinforcement of heteropatriarchy, and she argues the only way to combat heteropatriarchy is to cultivate a new paradigm, one not enforced by male dominance based on sexual desire but one cultivated by a communal alliance of women. By teaching Palahniuk's novel as an illustration of Jeffreys's theory, an instructor may demonstrate how *Snuff* is an extremely relevant novel about female exploitation and subsequent solidarity, especially if taught in conjunction with Stormy Daniels's accusations and the #MeToo movement.

Keywords: Chuck Palahniuk, Snuff, #MeToo, Lysistrata, Stormy Daniels

***

On May 13, 2019, Alyssa Milano and Waleisah Wilson proposed a sex strike that in many ways rivaled the one depicted in Aristophanes's *Lysistrata*. In a CNN op-ed piece entitled "Why the Time is Now for a #SexStrike," Milano and Wilson sound a call to all women to react via their physicality to recent state legislative maneuvers that have "chipped away at abortion rights . . . with the hopes of overturning Roe v. Wade." Milano and Wilson claim, "We must collectively reject these restrictions on our basic human rights and dignity in every way that we can. This flood of anti-abortion legislation is completely outrageous and an equally bold response is required. And, so, we call on all people whose rights are in danger to participate in a #SexStrike." To defend their position, Milano and Wilson pointed out that "Lysistratic protest is a longstanding, effective and empowering method to fight for change" and provide examples (Iroquois in the 1600s, Kenyans in 2009, and Columbians in 2011) to demonstrate how women have withheld sex to cause social, cultural, and political change. To emphasize their purpose, they assert, "A #SexStrike is a way to target straight, cisgender men so they may feel the physical consequences of our reproductive rights being systematically eliminated. This form of protest has the potential to raise the issue far beyond the usual groups engaged in debates about reproductive health. It's a way to ignite conversation and help everyone understand the gravity of the situation and the immediate need for swift action."[1] Reporting for *USA Today*, Sara M. Moniuszko, summarizes Milano and Wilson's strategy as simply "women protest controversial new anti-abortion laws by denying men sex."

Milano and Wilson's allusion to "Lysistratic protest" is extremely relevant. In "'Just hear that potty mouth!': An Argument for Sarah Ruden's Translation of *Lysistrata*," I maintain that Sarah Ruden's translation captures the essence of the joint Athenian and Spartan female rebellion against heteropatriarchy more effectively than any other version. In response to critics' claims that this translation is too low-brow because of the explicit sexual language, I counter that Ruden accurately contemporizes the Greek play by reflecting the personalities of many strong women in the media who advocate vehemently for feminist rights, many of whom are popular celebrities (several are comedians) who stood up against Hollywood sexual discrimination and harassment: "Ideally, they epitomize many tenets affiliated with third-wave feminism, and they could easily serve as Lysistratas in their own rights.

---

[1] Milano and Wilson contend, "Laws restricting abortion rights and access are a targeted attempt to erase decades of hard-fought gains for women's autonomy. A #SexStrike is another way for people who have the potential to get pregnant to call attention to this systematic onslaught and assert the power to change our own destinies."

Participants in the Women's March events since January 2017 or in the Me Too (#MeToo) movement since October 2017 have certainly demonstrated this courage and fortitude" (McCracken 616). Perhaps known mostly as a television and film actor, Milano certainly has spearheaded the #MeToo movement in what can now be perceived as fourth-wave feminism, differing from third-wave feminism primarily through its taking advantage of media and comparable agencies to advocate for women's rights. Personalities such as Milano possess rhetorical credibility partially because of their vast appeal. People identify them through their fictional personas. Likewise, I defend Ruden's transgressive presentation because of the appropriateness with which her translation imitates the behaviors, for better or worse, affiliated with the commonplace and the ordinary:

> Both Ruden and Lysistrata understand that they must battle fortified systems of power by appealing to basic human appetites, the instinctive drives that motivate toward change…Ruden speaks to the current generation of young women as well as to the new breed of classical scholars, ever mindful of the relationship between presentation and context. One might ask which translation is the closest to Aristophanes's original Greek; whether "dick," "prick," or "prong," for instance, is closest to *peos*? A response may be that the translators manipulate the raw material of the language to promote their agendas, politicizing the objective text for subjective reasons. In this regard, Ruden translates Aristophanes's language to address the rhetorical situation concerning a contemporary audience. (McCracken 617-18)

As I present in my article, Ruden adapts the message in *Lysistrata* by taking into account the pervasiveness of sexual innuendo and reference in a person's typical media consumption. I conclude, "Fortunately, most readers who maintain an open mind and suspend their moral prejudices see how Ruden's *Lysistrata* effectively advocates feminist values through a transgressive medium" (McCracken 618). Ruden, Milano, and other feminist activists understand the importance of adapting their rhetoric to the generally perceived normative, the average person who is continuously influenced by popular media (television, film, and music).

Chuck Palahniuk also understands this very well.

Case in point, Palahniuk's *Snuff* is more relevant now in a society hypersensitive to sexual harassment and women's reproductive rights than during its publication in 2008. Much has happened in ten years. Of all Palahniuk's novels, *Snuff* might be the one least likely taught in collegiate classes, particularly on predominantly conservative campuses. Besides expecting questions after students discover that the book is about a 600-man (strictly heterosexual) gangbang, instructors who attempt this feat should anticipate inquiries from administrators concerning the rationale for selecting a porn star's swan song (one full of sexual innuendos and references). Teaching *Snuff* is indeed a "gutsy" enterprise but one worth pursuing if couched within the appropriate context. One such approach is relating this novel to Stormy Daniels' (Stephanie Clifford's) private relationship with President Donald Trump and the proliferation of the #MeToo movement in American culture. Those unfamiliar with *Snuff* might hastily assume the novel is only about sex, as perhaps those misinformed about Stormy Daniels and #MeToo would only associate them with issues related to sexual misconduct. The same could be said for Ruden's *Lysistrata*, as this play could be hastily dismissed as soft porn, ignorantly pigeonholing the work as exploitative comedy. The truth is that these texts and this situation are much more about power than sex, and sex is merely a vehicle through which power is asserted and manipulated. This is precisely the point that Palahniuk addresses through *Snuff*.

By connecting *Snuff* with current political issues, as well as positioning it within various veins of feminist critical theory, students and administrators—and any others who see this as an anti-academic novel—will hopefully understand that this book, apparently about sex, is really not "about" sex. There is a lot more going in this story about Cassie Wright than carnal lust or cardinal sin. Feminist theory helps to illustrate this point. In *Anticlimax*, Sheila Jeffreys calls for a rethinking of heterosexuality in terms of its reinforcement of heteropatriarchy, and she argues the only way to combat heteropatriarchy is to cultivate a new paradigm, one not enforced by male dominance based on sexual desire but one cultivated by a communal alliance of women. Jeffreys contends, "No liberation is possible for women in a world in which inequality, and specifically the inequality of women, is sexy" (4). By teaching Palahniuk's novel as an illustration of Jeffreys's theory, an instructor may demonstrate how *Snuff* is an extremely relevant novel about female exploitation and subsequent solidarity, especially if taught in conjunction with the Stormy Daniels controversy and the #MeToo movement.

To reiterate, teaching *Snuff* is not, to apply a cliché, for instructors who are weak, are timid, or are faint of heart. I teach at a small liberal arts institution with approximately 1,200 students called Coker University. The school is transitioning from a college to a university (because of various Master's programs and other reasons), and although there is no religious denominational affiliation, the Southern small-town influence makes this a more conservative than liberal campus. To illustrate, I begin my article about

Ruden's *Lysistrata* with an anecdote describing the "civil disobedience" I encountered when I taught this play during an evening World Literature I class (603). I have taught *Snuff* three times, twice in what were American Novel classes, and another—much more productive because of the strategy I will report in this chapter—in a course devoted to Dirty Realism. When I taught the novel previously, I did not meet the same resistance that I faced in the world literature course concerning *Lysistrata*, but I failed to set up the novel well enough in advance to help them to understand the text's value, especially getting students prepared for the transgression. The students thought Palahniuk's story was amusing, but they did not really grasp the various nuances of meaning. They saw it as a sexual comedy, full of literary tricks and slapstick techniques along the lines of something presented on Adult Swim or in a Seth MacFarlane comedy.

In the Dirty Realism class during the spring of 2019, however, I made sure I frontloaded appropriately to help students recognize the irony in Palahniuk's story. Fortunately, the English program had recently changed its curriculum of upper-level offerings to include genre studies, literary themes, period/movement, and major author courses, eliminating the standard sequences of literary surveys and canon-driven 300 and 400-level classes. I was assigned to teach a movement course, so I chose American Dirty Realism, beginning with its pronouncement by Bill Buford in the eighth volume of *Granta* in the summer of 1983 (and revisited in the 19th volume of *Granta* during the fall of 1986) through definitions offered by Tobias Wolff, Tamas Dobozy, and others, and then through story collections by Raymond Carver, Bobbie Ann Mason, Charles Bukowski, and other writers affiliated with this movement.[2] For assessment related to *Snuff*, I required students to respond in

---

[2] Specifically, the class was ENG 320: Literary Period or Movement (Spring 2019): "ENG 320 Literary Period or Movement. While many authors are known for their individual work, some periods have spawned multiple authors working in relation to one another. Students in this course will examine the debates, dissensions, and collaborations of multiple authors active in a single period or school." For the course description, I provided this information:

> In *Hicks, Tribes, and Dirty Realists*, arguing American fiction has returned to a focus on realistic depictions of human experience, Robert Rebein writes, "Dirty Realism, as I would like to employ the term, refers to an effect in both subject matter and technique that is somewhere between the hard-boiled and the darkly comic. It refers to the impulse in writers to explore dark truths, to descend, as it were, into the darkest holes of society and what used to be called 'the soul of man.' Not the trailer parks and fern bars of minimalism, . . . but rather the more intense worlds of war, drug addiction, serious crime, prostitution, prison" (43). This definition differs in

forum posts to this prompt: "Explain how *Snuff* addresses female empowerment through sex." Students were to base their opinions upon selections of feminist criticism, information about transgressive fiction, and commentary about Stormy Daniels and #MeToo distributed prior to reading

---

degree from what has been considered the industry standard, editor Bill Buford's declaration in the summer 1983 publication of Granta concerning a new form of American writing: ". . . a curious, dirty realism about the belly-side of contemporary life, . . . so stylized and particularized—so insistently informed by a discomforting and sometimes elusive irony—that it makes the more traditional realistic novels of, say, Updike or Styron seem ornate, even baroque in comparison" (4). Announcing dirty realism as a "new fiction . . . emerging from America," Buford explains, It is instead a fiction of a different scope—devoted to the local details, the nuances, the little disturbances in language and gesture—and it is entirely appropriate that its primary form is the short story and that it is so conspicuously part of the American short story revival. But these are strange stories: unadorned, unfurnished, low-rent tragedies about people who watch day-time television, read cheap romances or listen to country and western music. They are waitresses in roadside cafés, cashiers in supermarkets, construction workers, secretaries and unemployed cowboys. They play bingo, eat cheeseburgers, hunt deer and stay in cheap hotels. They drink a lot and are often in trouble: for stealing a car, breaking a window, pickpocketing a wallet. (4) A widely cited definition attributed to Buford is from the back cover of the Penguin publication of the eighth issue of Granta: "Dirty Realism is the fiction of a new generation of American authors. They write about the belly-side of contemporary life—a deserted husband, an unwed mother, a car thief, a pickpocket, a drug addict—but they write about it with a disturbing detachment, at times verging on comedy. Understated, ironic, sometimes savage, but insistently compassionate, these stories constitute a new voice in fiction." For the most part, Rebein is identifying how dirty realism has drifted into the purview of transgressive fiction, portraying the "belly-side of contemporary life" as "darkly comic," a counterculture literary form that embodies the vulgar, profane, or obscene. ("ENG 320")

Last spring, I assigned stories from *Granta* (volume 8) and *Granta* (volume 19) by Richard Ford, Jayne Anne Phillips, and Louise Erdrich, and asked students to read selected stories from these collections: Raymond Carver's *Where I'm Calling From*, Bobbie Ann Mason's *Love Life*, Larry Brown's *Big Bad Love*, Dorothy Allison's *Trash*, Charles Bukowski's *General Tales of Ordinary Madness*, Denis Johnson's *Jesus' Son*, Junot Diaz's *Drown*, ZZ Packer's *Drinking Coffee Elsewhere*, and Chuck Palahniuk's *Make Something Up: Stories You Can't Unread*. I supplemented these readings with other primary and secondary texts related to minimalism, New Journalism, and Bizarro fiction (such as Carlton Mellick III's *I Knocked Up Satan's Daughter* or *The Haunted Vagina*). I planned the course so that students read *Snuff* while they were composing their course essays, mostly because Dirty Realism relates predominantly to short fiction.

Palahniuk's novel.³³ I also provided students with a section about *Snuff* from Douglas Keesey's *Understanding Chuck Palahniuk* (pages 81-87). Reading Palahniuk's short fiction immediately preceding *Snuff* helped to transition into this longer transgressive work.

We spent about a week and a half on transgressive fiction and Palahniuk's stories before hitting the novel. I summarized ideas from my book, *Chuck Palahniuk, Parodist*, especially from the chapter "'True Fact': Hyperreality in *Snuff*." I offered students particular selections from pieces defining transgressive writing, what Michael Silverblatt famously calls a characteristic of "the chic underground." In a 1996 *Atlantic* "Word Watch," Anne H. Soukhanov describes transgressive fiction as "a literary genre that graphically explores such topics as incest and other aberrant sexual practices, mutilation, the sprouting of sexual organs in various places on the human body, urban violence and violence against women, drug use, and highly dysfunctional family relationships, and that is based on the premises that knowledge is to be found at the edge of experience and that the body is the site for gaining knowledge . . ." (128). In her seminal 1995 *New York Times* article, Rene Chun comments, "Subversive, avant-garde, bleak, pornographic—and these are compliments. Such words are used to describe transgressive fiction, books pitched to young adults, written by authors descended from William Burroughs and the Marquis de Sade, that explore aberrant sexual practices, urban violence, drug use and dysfunctional families in graphic detail" (49). In "Chuck Palahniuk's *Beautiful You*, Alfred Kinsey's *Sexual Behavior in the Human Female*, and the Commodification of Female Sexual Desire," I write:

> transgressive writing reacts against established ethical and moral societal standards; exposing the darker shades, bleaker terrains, and rougher contours of humanity than presented in most mainstream fiction; focusing on the nihilistic and existential vicissitudes associated within the human experience. Transgressive fiction often includes content that is considered obscene, vulgar, and profane; and it frequently raises questions concerning what is proper or improper, acceptable or unacceptable, and even right or wrong. (McCracken 102)

---

³ I required each student to write a detailed forum post (2-3 double-spaced pages) in Blackboard, the course management system, in which he or she offered his or her opinion concerning how Palahniuk addressed female empowerment through sex based on selections from feminist criticism. If a student believed (based on personal ideology) the novel was too provocative to address in a high-stake graded project—as this had occurred when I taught *Snuff* previously—the low-stake informal writing assignment allowed for opinionated response.

I subsequently asked students to apply tenets of Dirty Realism and transgressive literature to these Palahniuk stories, all from *Make Something Up: Stories You Can't Unread*: "Cannibal," "How a Jew Saved Christmas," "How Monkey Got Married, Bought a Home, and Found Happiness in Orlando," "Knock-Knock," "Loser," "Red Sultan's Big Boy," "Romance," and The Toad Prince." Since the course met for 75 minutes twice a week, I required students to pick five or so stories on which to focus discussion. As expected, students were horrified by the adolescent's cunnilingus prowess ("Cannibal"), by the monster phallus ("The Toad Prince"), and by the horse bestiality ("Red Sultan's Big Boy"). After we parsed out the aspects of Dirty Realism in addition to the features of transgression, students were more receptive to digging into the texts for deeper meaning. This time was well spent because it set the table critically for academic analysis of *Snuff*.

On the first class day of four devoted to this novel, I introduced three important feminist theorists: Andrea Dworkin, Ariel Levy, and Jeffreys. This provided vital critical groundwork. I only gave students selections from their works. As several classes could be spent on all of the theoretical implications, I realized I had to be stingy on what was covered. In her famous feminist treatise *Intercourse*, amid comparison between Leo Tolstoy's sexual assaults upon his wife Sophie and the husband's sexual brutality of his spouse in *The Kreutzer Sonata*, Dworkin writes that the Russian author "locates his repulsion not in the woman's body, not in her inherent nature, but in sexual intercourse, the nature of the act: what it means; the inequality of the sexes intrinsic to it; its morbid consequences to the dignity and self-esteem of men" (8). She then claims Tolstoy was not averse to, perhaps even advocates, a cessation of sexual intercourse to eliminate the "repulsion" that seemingly causes men to act violently (8-10). I asked students to consider in particular Dworkin's provocative premise about female power: "The rage against women as a group is particularly located here: women manipulate men by manipulating men's sexual desire; these trivial, mediocre things (women) have real power over men through sex…This dominance of men by women is experienced by the men as real—emotionally real, sexually real, psychologically real; it emerges as the reason for the wrath of the misogynist. The whole world suffers . . . from the domination of men by women" (14-15).[4] I informed students that,

---

[4] Dworkin begins this passage, "For women, according to the killer/husband, virginity is the highest state, an ideal; and a fall from virginity is a fall into trivialization, into being used as a thing; one dresses up to the thing; one does not have a full humanity but must conform to the rituals and conventions of debasement as a sexual object. But this reduction of humanity into being an object for sex carries with it the power to dominate men because men want the object and the sex" (14).

generally (and this might be overstatement), Dworkin equates heterosexual intercourse with violent action, and as such, men and women compete for power through the sexual coitus.

I then presented students with a few passages from Levy. Palahniuk mentions this feminist activist explicitly in the fourth chapter, which is one of Shelia's narrative sections: "What to talk third-wave feminism, you could cite Ariel Levy and the idea that women have internalized male oppression. Going to spring break at Fort Lauderdale, getting drunk, and flashing your breasts isn't an act of personal empowerment. It's you, so fashioned and programmed by the construct of patriarchal society that you no longer know what's best for yourself. A damsel too dumb to even know she's in distress" (24). In *Female Chauvinist Pigs*, Levy contends women are just as culpable as men in the sexual commodification of female sexuality, women exploiting other women sexually within what she terms "raunch culture." After she describes her astonishment concerning how women have become feminist ideological hypocrites, Levy points out, "What was going on? . . . Only thirty years (my lifetime) ago, our mothers were 'burning their bras' and picketing Playboy, and suddenly we were getting implants and wearing the bunny logo as supposed symbols of our liberation" (3). Levy comments that her female friends are starting to identify with paraphernalia associated with the porn industry, purchasing porn merchandise, recognizing porn stars, and legitimizing porn ideology that was once offensive, amoral, and antisocial. In particular, I requested students to think about this paragraph:

> What was almost more surprising than the change itself were the responses I got when I started interviewing the men and—often—women who edit magazines like *Maxim* and make programs like *The Man Show* and *Girls Gone Wild*. This new raunch culture didn't mark the death of feminism, they told me; it was evidence that the feminist project had already been achieved. We'd *earned* the right to look at Playboy; we were *empowered* enough to get Brazilian bikini waxes. Women had come so far, I learned, we no longer needed to worry about objectification or misogyny. Instead, it was time for us to join the frat party of pop culture, where men had been enjoying themselves all along. If Male Chauvinist Pigs were men who regarded women as pieces of meat, we would outdo them and be Female Chauvinist Pigs: women who make sex objects of other women and of themselves. (3-4)

Levy concludes her introduction with illustrations of how porn has infiltrated the American mainstream, mentioning the notoriety of Pamela Anderson and Traci Lords, and asking this question, considering her mostly female audience: "And how is imitating a stripper or a porn star—a woman whose job is to imitate arousal in the first place—going to render us sexually liberated?" (4). Not surprisingly, students responded to the sections from Levy more easily than those from Dworkin, but I emphasized the purpose in looking at both was to consider the power exchange between men and women during heterosexual sexual relationships.

The last selection was from Jeffreys, and I connected this with a comment from Dworkin that, for women, "murder itself is the sex act or it is sexual climax" (7). This corresponds with Dworkin's comments about sex as a weapon and Levy's claims women use this weapon against themselves. Jeffreys writes:

> Defenders of pornography assert . . . that men want to be sex objects too. This shows a failure to grasp the politics of the process of objectification.... The problem with objectifying men for the consumption of women is that it is not sexy. In heterosexuality the attractiveness of men is based upon their power and status. Objectification removes the power and status.... Pornography is not egalitarian and gender-free. It is predicated upon the inequality of women and is the propaganda that makes that inequality sexy. (254)[5]

Through an almost "Lysistratic protest," Jeffreys lays out a course of action as a solution: "As women and as lesbians our hope lies only in other women. We must work towards the construction of homosexual desire and practice as a most important part of our struggle for liberation. However important heterosexual desire has been in our lives we will all have some experience of its opposite. We will have experience of sexual desire and practice which does not leave us feeling betrayed, a sexual desire and practice which eroticises mutuality and equality" (313). More important, and in a passage that seemingly contradicts Milano and Wilson's (as well as Lysistrata's) assertion, Jeffreys recommends perceiving sex in a different manner, an act promoting partnership rather than power, the opposite of the patriarchal "sacred ritual" fostering antagonism culminating in male dominance. Consequently, Jeffreys redefines the heterosexual/homosexual binary:

---

[5] Jeffreys continues, "For women to find passive, objectified men sexy in large enough numbers to make a pornography industry based upon such images viable, would require the reconstruction of women's sexuality into a ruling-class sexuality. In an egalitarian society objectification would not exist and therefore the particular buzz provided by pornography, the excitement of eroticized dominance for the ruling class, would be unimaginable" (254).

> The importance attached to sex defies rationality and can only be explained in this political way. But we can also choose, as many of us have done, to work towards homosexual desire if that suits our lives and relationships. We must remember that homosexual desire will not be recognised as ...'sex.' We do not even possess suitable words to describe it. (315)

Jeffreys is not proposing that women become lesbian or even bisexual, but she is requesting they see sexuality as not a male versus female adversarial gender war but in terms of a human plus human equitable alliance.[6]

Working through all of this, I asked students to reconsider Jeffreys's proposition that women cannot be liberated if they are continually placed in subordinate roles as objectified and commodified sexual entities. While they read *Snuff*, I urged them to think about her proposal that women "need to envision, and start to build, a world in which the connection of power difference and aggression to sexual feelings will be unimaginable" (4). In particular, I asked students to consider Jeffrey's assertion about homosexual desire: "This is desire which eroticises equality and mutuality,...When equality is exciting, not just at the level of theory but in love and sex, then the liberation of women becomes a real possibility" (4). Significantly, she argues that female sexual desire working against male sexual desire only privileges male heteropatriachy. There must be equality. I told them that *Snuff* responds to this need.

During the next meeting, I prompted students to discuss whether the first few chapters of *Snuff* enforce male domination or advocate female empowerment. Most of the students understood the buzzword "phallocentric," so they started from that point, teasing out if the novel supported heteropatriarchy. My expectation was that students would declare that men rule in this book about one woman having intercourse with 600 men. This could simply become a matter of overwhelming numbers, too

---

[6] Jeffreys broaches this concept, explaining this is really a matter pertaining to power relationships:
> Readers who consider themselves to be heterosexual will probably be wondering whether homosexual desire can fit into an opposite-sex relationship. In a society which was not founded upon the subordination of women there would be no reason why it should not. But we do not live in such a society. We live in a society organized around heterosexual desire, around otherness and power difference. It is difficult to imagine what shape a woman's desire for a man would take in the absence of eroticized power difference since it is precisely this which provides the excitement of heterosexuality today. (316)

many men and one woman, who did not even have a chapter of her own, therefore no voice in her own story. Moreover, I anticipated a conservative stance from some that pornography is inherently anti-female and a genre mostly consumed by males. I attempted to counter this by showing students how pornography has infiltrated the American mainstream. Taking advantage of resources online, I displayed several short, easily accessible articles from *USA Today* that document the affair between Stormy Daniels (portrayed mostly through her porn persona) and President Trump.[7] Naturally, students had heard of this affair that was leaked in January of 2018, and although they were not (nor was I) familiar with all of the intricacies concerning the situation, they understood that the controversy is not so much a moral one about marital infidelity as it is about a cover-up related to money given to the woman not to broadcast anything about the one-time sexual encounter. They noticed, via the articles, that Clifford signed a nondisclosure agreement but subsequently wanted to speak publicly about the affair. Students also read that President Trump is confronting a similar situation with former Playboy Playmate Karen McDougal. I turned class discussion toward the relevance of Clifford/Daniels being a porn star, looking at this incident as a potential #MeToo issue in that the male (President Trump) represents privileged heteropatriarchy whereas the female (Stormy Daniels) is apparently the harassed victim.

I asked students if they knew of any other porn stars (recognizing no one would probably admit openly to viewing porn). Outside of class (not during the meeting), students said they identified one true porn actor, Jenna Jameson (although they thought she was an "old" porn star), but they also cited celebrities who would likely be insulted if they were placed in this category: Kim Kardashian, Jenny McCarthy, Charissa Thompson, Pamela Anderson, and other media personalities who are not actually porn stars but who, to support Levy's assertions, assume identifiable personas usually affiliated with sex entertainers. Students thought "leaked" Internet videos and provocative photo images suggested these women did not fear displaying their sexual sides publicly. I told the students that First Lady Melania Trump, a former fashion model, has posed in photos promoting her physical attractiveness, and Hillary Clinton's presidential spouse reputably had extramarital affairs

---

[7] These *USA Today* articles are Doug Stanglin's "Porn Star Stormy Daniels' Alleged Affair with Trump Takes New Twist with Old Interview," Jessica Estepa's "Meet 19 Women Who Claim Affairs with Trump or Accuse Him of Unwanted Advances," and an Associated Press (although published in *USA Today*) piece entitled "Trump Seeks Arbitration in Stormy Daniels Case."

with Paula Jones and Gennifer Flowers (who both posed in the sex magazine *Penthouse*) and "sexual relations" with an intern named Monica Lewinsky. I stressed that sometimes the vision of what is truly porn becomes blurred, as the distinction between soft core and glamour shot is often hard to judge. To illustrate, I showed students the controversial Alabama sorority recruitment video that has been criticized for its soft porn imagery.[8] This video is not unlike many recruiting videos that sororities use to get pledges, but students usually agree that some of the images could be construed as sexually charged yet not intended for sexual enticement.

To tie all of this together, I requested students suspend any prejudices that they had initially about *Snuff*'s subject matter pertaining to sex and about pornography. I wanted them to compare Cassie Wright to Stormy Daniels, to perceive them as something other than sexual commodities, and to consider how these two women were fighting deeply rooted heteropatriarchal ideology so that they might have the freedom to articulate their own stories, to express themselves as they wished with impunity. I recommended that students access Stormy Daniels's *Wikipedia* page to see how her life compares with her fictional counterpart, and I advised them to peruse the *Wikipedia* page devoted to Stormy Daniels's relationship with President Trump to assess through the documented "facts" if she has been harassed or discriminated against.[9] I requested students to also consider Dworkin's and Levy's positions within the context of the novel, especially in terms of power and control. In one sense, if Dworkin is correct, the entire story documents the heinously brutal sexual assault of Cassie Wright by 600 men. In another sense, if Levy is right, Sheila might be exploiting Cassie Wright's sexuality for her own opportunistic agenda. I emphasized that they might find that Palahniuk is playing with stereotypes and prejudices and will eventually offer them something in the middle, more aligned with Jeffrey's call for a new way, a different paradigm, through which to view sexual politics. I reinforced the crucial premise that this novel, full of transgressive descriptions of sex, is fundamentally about power through heteropatriarchal practices of sex. I prepared them not to be surprised at the end if they change their opinions about what Palahniuk might be asking them to consider about the relationship between sexuality and empowerment.

---

[8] This video is available on *YouTube* as "Alabama Alpha Phi 2015—Controversial Sorority Rush Video." Discussion of the video is included in Kristen Rein's "U of Alabama Sorority Criticized for Recruitment Video" and A. L. Bailey's "'Bama Sorority Video Worse for Women than Donald Trump."

[9] These *Wikipedia* sites are "Stormy Daniels" and "Stormy Daniels-Donald Trump Scandal."

When I addressed *Snuff* directly, I focused on particular sections related to the extensive critical preparation. I have learned the hard way that I cannot really just ask open-ended questions such as "So, what do you think about this novel?" or "What really caught your attention while you were reading?" I spent so much time leading students to this place in the class that I could not be general, vague, or ambiguous about my intentions when we finally got to the close readings of passages. These were the three important points that I wanted covered: Branch Bacardi's rape of Cassie Wright, Sheila's manipulation of Cassie Wright, and Cassie Wright's empowerment at the end of the novel. My goal was to tie these points to the feminist criticism and ultimately to apply the fictional ideas with those in reality, particularly Stormy Daniels and those associated with #MeToo. I must admit that there were digressions given to Sheila's commentaries concerning maverick star of the gangbang Annabel Chong (Grace Quek), Roman nymphomaniac empress Messalina, and the trivia related to the motion picture industry woven within the fabric of the story. Because of time limitations, I had to redirect attention toward the three points.

First, I posed the question about whether Branch Bacardi raped Cassie Wright. In several places in the story, there are clues that she willingly asked Branch Bacardi (actually named Irwin) to tape their sexual intercourse, and this tape became her first porn appearance that launched what became a prosperous career in adult entertainment. After reading the first third of the novel, students thought, taking Palahniuk's bait, that the crux of the story was Cassie Wright's death wish to provide for her "porn baby," most likely Mr. 72 (Darin Johnson) (61). Redirecting the focus, I asked students to remember Dworkin's argument that sexual intercourse is fundamentally a violent action, the empowered male assaulting the subordinate female, harboring resentment that the female, through sexual desire, instigates the event. According to Dworkin, men realize that women have real sexual power over them, and this resentment fuels male aggression toward females. In chapter ten, Mr. 72 provides Cassie Wright's biography, telling Mr. 137 and Mr. 600 about Cassie seeking help from her parents in Montana. Her initial film entitled *World Whore One* was famous, but she needed help with the "love child," as Mr. 137 calls it, conceived during its production (58-59). After getting caught masturbating to a Cassie Wright film on his computer, Mr. 72 states his adopted mother revealed that Cassie was his birth mother (87). In chapter fifteen, through obvious answers to her questions, Sheila indirectly tells Mr. 137 that Cassie was relegated to a life in porn after being raped by Branch Bacardi: "The sick fuck who talked her into this awful business? The living piece of shit who slipped her Demerol and Drambuie, then set up cameras and fucked her from every angle?" (92-93). In chapter seventeen, Mr. 137 confronts Branch Bacardi by letting him know he knows his intentions: "Why not drug your son? You already drugged his mother . . ." (102). In

Chapter nineteen, Sheila calls Branch Bacardi a "rapist" who wanted the baby aborted (115). However, in Chapter twenty-two, Branch Bacardi offers his side, stating that Cassie Wright actually planned the filming: "It was Cassie wanted to shoot a porn loop to escape her folks' house. Cassie asked could I score her something to help her relax" (140). More importantly, he tells Mr. 72 that Cassie wants to die through cyanide poisoning: "it's what she wants most" (140). Nonetheless, Branch Bacardi tells Mr. 72 the true story in chapter thirty-two—how Cassie Wright planned to attend drama school, remembering how she had said sarcastically that "maybe if she was stupid and desperate, really clutching at straws and emotionally needy, utterly destroyed," she would have stayed with him. He admits: "If you got to know, Cassie never planned to make that first movie" (186). This testimony confirms that Cassie was raped.

Second, I proposed the question about whether Sheila had manipulated Cassie Wright. In many places in the novel, Sheila seems to care for Cassie Wright in her job as wrangler, but this transitions to hatred and then to admiration. I have noticed that students seem to miss that Shelia is indeed the catalyst for the 600-man gangbang. Most students are astonished that Sheila is Cassie's child and has arranged this potential snuff film as a devious plot to collect the insurance money. I reminded students that Keesey quotes Palahniuk as claiming Sheila's sections were added to "make the book less 'claustrophobic,'" and Sheila's nine chapters are crucial to interpreting *Snuff* as a reaction against heteropatriarchy (85). I asked students to remember Levy's claim that women propagate the misconception that they are self-empowered through self-objectification and by promoting the commodification of other females through raunch culture, which certainly includes participating in pornography. In chapter eight, Sheila admits that she seemingly stalks Cassie Wright to "pitch" the concept of a record-setting porn extravaganza based on "a Nazi angle" affiliated with Hitler's manufacturing of blow-up sex dolls (48-49). This is when Cassie admits to being a "mom," and Sheila provides the incentive that the project would "make a pile of money for that baby" (49). In chapter twenty, Sheila almost enjoys drawing blood as she helps Cassie Wright wax her pubic hair. Ironically, after giving Sheila celebrity beauty secrets that inflict self-pain, Cassie says, "Didn't your momma teach anything?" and admits confidentially that she did not "set out to be a porn star" (123; 126). In chapter twenty-eight, Sheila reveals that she is Cassie's daughter and confesses that Cassie recognized her a such immediately, which suggests that Sheila has knowingly coerced her mother into a potential death act and Cassie is a feminist martyr through Sheila's betrayal (176). Sheila rationalizes that she is one who has been manipulated: "All along, the woman knew who I was. Who she really was. She played along, knowing she would die. Cassie Wright would willingly fuck six hundred pud-pullers to make me rich . . . That *bitch*" (184). In chapter thirty-two, Sheila's scheme and Branch

Bacardi's ploy come together, as a woman and a man attempt to exploit Cassie Wright sexually. Branch sees Cassie awaiting him "as a blow-up sex-doll version of herself" and considers the reason why he gave her the life-changing betaketamine and Demerol cocktail: "Because I loved her so much" (185). This is only nostalgic self-deception to justify his killing her with the cyanide. Sheila's revelation only exposes her own self-loathing and self-pity.

Third, I proposed the question if Cassie Wright is ultimately redeemed. Both Sheila and Branch Bacardi seem to love her, but this does not forgive (to return to Dworkin's and Levy's arguments) their exploitation of her. I asked students to remember Jeffreys' claim that giving into heterosexual desire only reinforces the dominance of what is at its core really heteropatriarchal power, and an alternative is to implement a homosexual desire that defuses the source of that power. Instead of following Lysistrata's, as well as Milano and Wilson's, call for a sex strike, Cassie Wright works the opposite direction, participating in sex for advantage. This is an extremely important point: Cassie Wright puts into action the binary of Milano and Wilson's "equally bold response" against heteropatriarchy to achieve the same goal, empowerment through more sex rather than less sex. Similar to Stormy Daniels, Cassie Wright understands the political implications of sexual intercourse. Likewise, comparable to Daniels, Cassie Wright reassesses her situation and attempts to change the original social contract. After Cassie acknowledges her understanding of the types of exploitation working against her, she decides to counterattack, and this is through her taking control of her situation. Sheila serves as the facilitator during the sexual exercise of getting men to Cassie Wright for at least one minute of sexual penetration. While the men are in what is comparable to a basement bullpen for the athletic main event upstairs, movies of Cassie play on monitors. These films display Cassie's life (presumably from around twenty to her early forties, her current age). In chapter three, there are details of Cassie's "comeback" when she might have participated in, by porn standards, less-than-prestigious fetish and bestiality productions, but, for the most part, Cassie enjoyed stardom in the porn business (16). There are references to her preparing for her roles through conscientious attention to real-life detail, as when she shadowed an endocrinologist for a film, and she inserts Kegel-exercise stones and other "vaginal weights" to strengthen her muscles for the impending sexual competition (9; 71; 73).

Worth noting, maybe emphasizing, Palahniuk published *Snuff* well before #MeToo, but Cassie Wright is a dedicated professional who performs in an entertainment industry that is unquestionably controlled by heteropatriarchy. In the mainstream entertainment industry, Milano, Rose McGowan, Ashley Judd, and other actors deemed "The Silence Breakers" were awarded *Time*'s

Person of the Year for 2017 (Zacharek, Dockterman, and Edwards).[10] In a similar act of rebellion against heteropatriarchy, Stormy Daniels and other women comparably exposed President Trump for sexual indiscretions. All of the parodies of mainstream films and the references to actual celebrities in *Snuff* compare, in 2019, to highlight the prevalence of heteropatriarchy in popular media. Students reading *Snuff* currently might not realize that Palahniuk was almost looking forward in this novel, predicting the "Lysistratic protest" of strong women who helped to precipitate what has become fourth-wave feminism.

I wanted students to recognize that Cassie Wright is such a strong woman. Undoubtedly, there are instances in the novel when she takes charge of the situation. In chapter twenty-six, when Mr. 72 realizes he is not having sexual intercourse with his mother and begins thrashing wildly, Cassie sarcastically replies to her production crew, "You guys getting this?" (168). In chapter thirty-four, when Branch Bacardi swallows the cyanide, Cassie Wright repeats, "Are you getting this?" (192). As two students in my ENG 320 pointed out astutely, Branch Bacardi exemplifies heteropatriarchal control recognized by Dworkin, Levy, and Jeffreys. As literally the last man standing for sex, Mr. 600, Branch Bacardi exerts his dominance—heterosexual male control—over the situation by thwarting Cassie Wright's spectacular moment, trying to take authority from her. Unbelievably, she has had 599 sex acts prior to this moment, and this is Branch Bacardi's chance, perhaps his last chance, to take the spotlight away from her. Courageously, Cassie Wright refuses to relinquish power. She squats over the "stiff blue erection" and firmly impales herself upon what is remarkably "a big dick" (193). In this circumstance, description of this penis is warranted to accentuate the phallocentric magnitude of both the literal physicality as well as the symbolic meaning. Similar to Stephanie Clifford (as a person, not a porn persona) and those affiliated with #MeToo, Cassie Wright reacts against a representative of heteropatriarchy: "Upstage me . . . you prick piece of shit. . . . You stole my biggest scene, you rat bastard" (193). Incredibly, she refuses to pander to phallocentrism. She has control.

When Cassie Wright and Branch Bacardi are melded together through the electrical charge of the cardiac defibrillators, they achieve consummate

---

[10] 10. People profiled in the *Time* issue are Isabel Pascual, Adama Iwu, Ashley Judd, Susan Fowler, Taylor Swift, Alyssa Milano, Tarana Burke, Selma Blair, Sara Gelser, Lindsay Meyer, Sandra Pezqueda, Rose McGowan, Wendy Walsh, Lindsey Reynolds, Juana Melara, Sandra Muller, Terry Crews, Celeste Kidd, Jessica Cantlon, Megyn Kelly, Jane Merrick, Zelda Perkins, Terry Reintke, Bex Bailey, Amanda Schmitt, Blaise Godbe Lipman, in addition to a few anonymous women.

equality—literally and metaphorically. As the "billion volts of power" unite them, neither person is privileged nor disadvantaged, assailant nor victim. The product is only a neutral signifier, a "human X" (196) that is connected by genitalia. This might not be exactly what Jeffreys had in mind, but when she states that homosexual desire (referring to equality through similarity) may not be recognizable, something indescribable, but this human X might offer a visual model of Jeffreys's paradigm. Moreover, Sheila may view the human signification of her parents' bonding as the union of love and sex, something that enables her at the end of this novel to become "real" by exposing her "secret name" (197). To apply Jeffreys' words, Cassie Wright's action has prompted the liberation of Sheila to become a real possibility. To make this more authentic, Palahniuk could have revealed Cassie's true name. Just as "Stormy Daniels" is a stage moniker, "Cassie Wright" is only a porn persona. Keesey points out the performance appellation is taken from Stephen King's *Carrie* as Carrie White is mistakenly called Cassie Wright by her school principal (82). Moreover, in terms of empowerment, instead of Cassie Wright's death—the purpose of a "snuff" film—she experiences something comparable to a feminist apotheosis, a spiritual rebirth, which refutes Dworkin's claim that the sexual climax is death. In *Snuff, la petite mort* takes on new meaning. I wanted students to see Cassie Wright as gaining complete redemption at the end of *Snuff*.

In her review of the novel, "Love the Ones You're With," Lucy Ellmann blasts Palahniuk. She contends, "What the hell is going on? The country that produced Melville, Twain and James now venerates King, Crichton, Grisham, Sebold and Palahniuk. Their subjects? Porn, crime, pop culture and an endless parade of out-of-body experiences. Their methods? Cliché, caricature and proto-Christian morality. Props? Corn chips, corpses, crucifixes. The agenda? Deceit: a dishonest throwing of the reader to the wolves. And the result? Readymade Hollywood scripts" (27). She sees little literary, critical, or aesthetic value in his writing. Furthermore, she predicts *Snuff* will also have little future worth: "Instead of any real creative effort, Palahniuk chucks at us every bit of porno-talk he can muster. But not in a good way. This is no celebration of a field in which America excels—the hatching of new vocabulary—but an exercise in deadening the English language. Johnny One-Note, this book is shooting blanks. Alienation is soooooo 20th century" (27). On June 12, 2019, another advocate of #MeToo, Mira Sorvino testified during a news conference at the New York State Capitol about her own survival as a victim of date rape. As Maria Puente, Jon Campbell, and Joseph Spector report, "Sorvino is one of the most prominent leaders of the #MeToo and #TimesUp movements to call out sexual misconduct in Hollywood. She has previously alleged she's been sexually harassed, sexually battered and assaulted and even gagged with a condom during an audition when she was a teenager." Ellmann is simply incorrect in her condemnation of Palahniuk as a writer whom she claims exhibits a "lack of artistry" and offers "feeble irony" (27). Just the opposite. During a time when #MeToo advocates such as Milano and Sorvino are in the news reacting against toxic masculinity associated with heteropatriarchal power, Palahniuk's novel still addresses pertinent social, cultural, and political isses more than a decade after its publication. No, Ms. Ellmann, Palahniuk is not a "Johnny One-Note." In fact—"true fact," even, per the refrain in *Snuff*—he seems to address controversial issues that are soooooo 21st century.

Works Cited

"Alabama Alpha Phi 2015—Controversial Sorority Rush Video." *YouTube*, uploaded by Unlimited News, 17 Aug. 2015, www.youtube.com/watch?v=3 QtENKvfxXQ. Accessed 13 June 2019.

Allison, Dorothy. *Trash*. Plume, 2002.

Bailey, A. L. "'Bama Sorority Video Worse for Women than Donald Trump." *AL.com*, Alabama Media Group, 14 Aug. 2014, www.al.com/opinion/index. ssf/2015/08/bama_sorority_ video_worse_for.html. Accessed 13 June 2019.

Brown, Larry. *Big Bad Love*. Vintage, 1990.

Buford, Bill. Editorial. "Dirty Realism: New Writing from America." *Granta*, no. 8, Summer 1983, pp. 4-5.

Bukowski, Charles. *General Tales of Ordinary Madness*. 1983. Virgin, 2009.

Carver, Raymond. *Where I'm Calling From*. Vintage, 1989.

Chun, Rene. "Naked Lunch and Dinner." *New York Times*, 23 Apr. 1995, pp. 49, 52.

Diaz, Junot. *Drown*. Riverhead, 1996.

Dobozy, Tamas. *Towards a Definition of Dirty Realism*. Dissertation, U. of British Columbia, 2000, open.library.ubc.ca/cIRcle/collections/ubctheses/ 831/ items/1.0089734. Accessed 13 June 2019.

Dworkin, Andrea. *Intercourse*. Free Press, 1987.

Ellmann, Lucy. "Love the Ones You're With." *The New York Times*, 8 June 2008, p. 27.

Estepa, Jessica. "Meet 19 Women Who Claim Affairs with Trump or Accuse Him of Unwanted Advances." *USA Today*, 20 Mar. 2018, www.usatoday.com/story/ news/politics/onpolitics/2018/03/20/meet-19-women-who-claim-affairs-tru mp-accuse-him-unwanted-advances/443685002/. Accessed 13 June 2019.

Granta: Dirty Realism: New Writing from America 8. Penguin, 1983.

Granta: More Dirt: The New American Fiction 19. Penguin, 1986.

Jeffreys, Sheila. *Anticlimax: A Feminist Perspective on the Sexual Revolution*. Women's Press, 1990.

Johnson, Denis. *Jesus' Son*. Picador, 1992.

Keesey, Douglas. "Porn Bodies and Romantic Myths: *Snuff, Tell-All, Beautiful You*." *Understanding Chuck Palahniuk*. U of South Carolina P, 2016, pp. 81-100.

Levy, Ariel. *Female Chauvinist Pigs: Women and the Rise of Raunch Culture.* Free Press, 2005.

Mason, Bobbie Ann. *Love Life.* Harper Perennial, 1989.

McCracken, David. "Chuck Palahniuk's *Beautiful You*, Alfred Kinsey's *Sexual Behavior in the Human Female*, and the Commodification of Female Sexual Desire." *Studies in Popular Culture*, vol. 39, no. 1, 2016, pp. 101-22.

——. "ENG 320 Course Policies." ENG 320, Coker College. Received 15 Jan. 2019. Course handout.

——. "'Just hear that potty mouth!': An Argument for Sarah Ruden's Translation of *Lysistrata.*" *Neohelicon*, vol. 45, no. 2, 2018, pp. 603-19.

——. "'True Fact': Hyperreality in *Snuff.*" *Chuck Palahniuk, Parodist: Postmodern Irony in Six Transgressive Novels.* McFarland, 2016, pp. 37-53.

Mellick III, Carlton. *The Haunted Vagina.* Eraserhead, 2005.

——. *I Knocked Up Satan's Daughter.* Eraserhead, 2011.

Milano, Alyssa, and Waleisah Wilson. "Why the Time is Now for #SexStrike." *CNN Opinion*, 13 May 2019, www.cnn.com/2019/05/13/opinions/alyssa-milano-sex-strike-now/index.html. Accessed 13 June 2019.

Moniuszko, Sara M. "Alyssa Milano Explains Sex Strike: 'Extreme Response' Was Needed To Get National Attention." *USA Today*, 14 May 2019, www.usatoday.com/story/life/people/2019/05/14/alyssa-milano-explains-contro versial-sex-strike-op-ed/3664792002/. Accessed 13 June 2019.

Packer, ZZ. *Drinking Coffee Elsewhere.* Riverhead, 2005.

Palahniuk, Chuck. "Cannibal." *Make Something Up*, pp. 80-88.

——. "How a Jew Saved Christmas." *Make Something Up*, pp. 310-18.

——. "How Monkey Got Married, Bought a Home, and Found Happiness in Orlando." *Make Something Up*, pp. 18-27.

——. "Knock-Knock." *Make Something Up*, 1-9.

——. "Loser." *Make Something Up*, 40-49.

——. *Make Something Up: Stories You Can't Unread.* Doubleday, 2015.

——. "Red Sultan's Big Boy." *Make Something Up*, pp. 50-69.

——. "Romance." *Make Something Up*, 70-79.

——. *Snuff.* Doubleday, 2008.

——. "The Toad Prince." *Make Something Up*, 136-45.

Puente, Maria, Jon Campbell, and Joseph Spector. "Tearful Mira Sorvino Says 'I Was Date-Raped,' Advocates for Statute of Limitations Changes." *USA Today*, 12 June 2019, www.usatoday.com/story/life/2019/06/12/mira-sorv ino-i-date-raped-argues-for-new-statute-of-limitations-laws/1432440001/. Accessed 13 June 2019.

Rebein, Robert. *Hicks, Tribes, and Dirty Realists: American Fiction after Postmodernism.* UP of Kentucky, 2001.

Rein, Kristen. "U of Alabama Sorority Criticized for Recruitment Video." *USA Today*, 18 Aug. 2015, www.usatoday.com/story/news/nation-now/2015/08/ 18/university-alabama-criticized-racially-homogeneous-recruitment-video /31900097/. Accessed 13 June 2019.

Ruden, Sarah, translator. *Lysistrata*. By Aristophanes. *The Norton Anthology of World Literature*, edited by Martin Puchner et al., 3rd ed., vol. A, Norton, 2012, pp. 823-62.

Silverblatt, Michael. "Shock Appeal—Who Are These Writers, and Why Do They Want to Hurt Us?: The New Fiction of Transgression." *The Los Angeles Times*, 1 August 1993, p. 7.

Soukhanov, Anne H. "Word Watch." *The Atlantic*, December 1996, p.128.

Stanglin, Douglas. "Porn Star Stormy Daniels' Alleged Affair with Trump Takes New Twist with Old Interview," *USA Today*, 18 Jan. 2018, www.usatoday.com/story/news/2018/01/18/porn-stars-alleged-affair-trump-takes-new-twist-old-interview/1043583001/. Accessed 13 June 2019.

"Stormy Daniels." *Wikipedia: The Free Encyclopedia*, Wikimedia Foundation, 13 June 2019, en.wikipedia.org/wiki/Stormy_Daniels. Accessed 13 June 2019.

"Stormy Daniels-Donald Trump Scandal." *Wikipedia: The Free Encyclopedia*, Wikimedia Foundation, 26 May 2019. Accessed 13 June 2019.

"Trump Seeks Arbitration in Stormy Daniels Case." *USA Today*, 2 Apr. 2018, www.usatoday.com/story/news/politics/2018/04/03/trump-seeks-arbitration-stormy-daniels-case/480746002/. Accessed 13 June 2019.

Wolff, Tobias. Introduction. *The Picador Book of Contemporary American Stories*, edited by Wolff, Pan, 1993, pp. vii-xii.

Zacharek, Stephanie, Eliana Dockterman, and Haley Sweetland Edwards. "The Silence Breakers: *Time* Person of the Year 2017." *Time.com*, Time USA, time.com/time-person-of-the-year-2017-silence-breakers/. Accessed 13 June 2019.

Chapter 8

The United States of Caucasia: Teaching Palahniuk in the Classroom to Raise Awareness of the Dangers of White Anxiety in America

Andrew Burlingame

Catholic University

Abstract: In Chuck Palahniuk's recent work, *Adjustment Day*, the United States government is overthrown and reorganized by a coup that is motivated by the working class and its undercurrent relationship to white anxiety. White nationalists like Richard Spencer condemn diversity in America as "away of bringing to an end a nation and a culture," while advocating for a white ethno-state which he calls the "grand goal" that would establish "a homeland for white people." Palahniuk's characters suggest otherwise. Once the country is redistributed into regions determined by race and sexual orientation, Caucasia founders, in part, because whites no longer have scapegoats to excuse societal problems for which they are responsible. In the age of Trump with the emboldened presence of the Alt-Right, *Adjustment Day* would serve as an excellent resource to contextualize and historicize the rhetoric of white nationalists being put into action by linking it to the various attempts to incriminate, scapegoat, and seek to segregate Whites from ethnic and religious minorities in America. William Frye Jacobson, John Higham, David H. Bennett, and Philip Jenkins, whose works examine nativism, white supremacy, and racism, and right-wing extremism throughout American history, will be paired with the novel create a course plan about the evolution of the concept of whiteness, focusing on mistreatment by white America of various ethnic white minorities as well as the political subjugation of religious minorities during the 19th and 20th centuries. The synthesis of the novel with the historical record and theoretical texts will illuminate the present moment of white anxiety.

Keywords: Chuck Palahniuk, Adjustment Day, Nativism, White Anxiety, Immigration, Insurrection

***

When Mexico sends its people, they're not sending their best...They're sending people that have lots of problems, and they're bringing those problems with them. They're bringing drugs. They're bringing crime. They're rapists. And some, I assume, are good people.

– Donald Trump, 2015

Ireland and Ulster "discharge their jails of the vilest part of their subjects and...transport shiploads of wretches, too worthless for the old world, to taint and corrupt the infancy of the new."

– Benjamin Franklin, 1787

In an America living in the aftermath of an armed insurrection of the United States Capitol on January 6, 2021, the premise of Chuck Palahniuk's *Adjustment Day* in which a coup led by white supremacists to overthrow the U.S. government seems even more prescient now than in 2018 at the time of its publication. Because the violence on January 6, 2021, occurred at the hands of rabid Trump supporters and white nationalists, it would be hard to argue that white supremacy and white nationalism are not on the rise, especially with Nazis flaunting their hatred and bigotry in the streets. Novels such as *Adjustment Day* can be taught in the classroom in conjunction with history texts to supplement an understanding of the long history of racism, nativism, religious intolerance, and the persecution and scapegoating of the "other" by the dominant white class in America. *Adjustment Day* and other similar works of fiction can also teach students what happens when a white utopia or "ethno-state" is finally achieved and there are no longer any "others" to blame for society's problems.

Chuck Palahniuk wrote *Adjustment Day* following the 2016 presidential election. The novel takes place in the near future in the United States in a society on the verge of collapse as various groups seem to be incapable of living together peacefully, leaving the country poised for another World War as Congress prepares to reinstate the draft. A mysterious figure, Talbott Reynolds, emerges to hatch a plan to solve this national crisis.

As the United States government prepares for war, a blue-black book called *Adjustment Day*, authored by Reynolds, begins to circulate across the country. Young men all across America are carrying around this mysterious book with cryptic messages and quotations scrawled in the pages. Just when it appears that virile male youths are doomed to an early grave in WWIII, these disaffected members of society rise up to turn the tables on the government, slaughtering all of the nation's elites in a violent and murderous coup. The main targets for extermination are the educated and the powerful: professors, politicians, and the media.

With the elites successfully decimated, the new ruling class of workers emerges as the interim government. The impending World War has been averted, but now the new government needs a solution to the diversity crisis in the "former…disunited states" of America (Palahniuk 256). To combat this problem, the new ruling class, under the direction of Talbott Reynolds, divides the country into three distinct colonies based upon ethnicity and sexual preferences: Caucasia, Blacktopia, Gaysia. Anyone not fitting into these three groups, including Latinos, Asians, and Jews, among others, must leave the country voluntarily or forcibly.

Blacktopia, a state comprised entirely of individuals of African descent, thrives as blacks have the ability to run their own society free from white suppression. Their true genius comes out as their society develops new technology and discovers cures for deadly diseases. The second new political zone, Gaysia, turns into something comparable to a *Handmaid's Tale* society. Due to obstacles with reproduction, the lesbians are forced to become surrogates and the gay men are forced to provide the sperm in mandatory sperm drives. The final territory, Caucasia, is completely dysfunctional. This society reverts into a feudal state. With no one to scapegoat for their problems, the colony descends into chaos as a lack of resources ultimately leads to cannibalism.

Palahniuk's novel, specifically his treatment of Caucasia, highlights a key aspect of American culture: what today has become known as white nationalism. The face of white nationalism during the Trump Era, Richard Spencer, is a firm believer in the idea of a white ethno-state like Caucasia, a community where the white race would hypothetically thrive once it separated itself from ethnic and sexual minorities. Spencer condemned diversity in America as "a way of bringing to an end a nation and a culture" while advocating for a white ethno-state which he calls the "grand goal" that would establish "a homeland for white people" (Grinberg and McLaughlin). But Spencer is just the most recent figure advocating for a utopia for whites while blaming the "other" for society's flaws and problems.

Because of the increased prominence of figures like Spencer and the crisis over American democracy and identity created by those who ascribe to and even exceed the conspiracy-driven ethos of white nationalism, it is important that historians and their students work together to unpack the deep roots of these ideologies and how they evolve. In a classroom, virtual or brick-and-mortar, *Adjustment Day* can serve as an unexpected entry point to a conversation about an understanding of history that departs from some of the more positivist, entrenched narratives about America and American identity. Because *Adjustment Day* is fiction, students may be more willing to suspend disbelief and engage more openly with ideas about white anxiety and its relationship to American identity. A short writing assignment to prime students for discussion might be: "How do Palahniuk's depictions of Blacktopia and Caucasia fail to square with white supremacist ideology and how does this complicate a fundamental definition of an "American" being coded and normed from an implicit understanding whiteness?"

In opening the discussion of Palahniuk's novel, we could address the idea that, since the country's inception, the white dominant class in America has always persecuted and scapegoated the newly arrived threat: immigrants of different religious, ethnic, and ultimately racial backgrounds. These newcomers have been blamed for increases in crime, bringing disease and illness, remaining loyal only to their former homelands, trying to change American culture and values, and generally, degrading the moral fabric of the country. These immigrants were and continue to be framed by the dominant white class as the most perilous and impending threat to the country, that is, until a newer, even more "other" group comes along to replace them. Once this occurs, the former group slowly becomes assimilated as part of the dominant white class, subsequently engaging in the nativist attacks to which they were once subjected. Matthew Frye Jacobson, a leading scholar in the subfield of whiteness studies, highlights this cyclical trend in which older immigrants and their descendants condemn "to everlasting inferiority the immigrants of a latter decade" (156). While blacks, sexual minorities, and other such groups have also obviously been persecuted and scapegoated by the white dominant class throughout America's history, I will be focusing on the mistreatment of immigrants in my argument, touching upon these other oppressed groups at times as the evolution of the term "white" evolves over generations. In Palahniuk's novel, groups such as Asians and Latinos are cast out of the new society, not fitting racially into the white ethno-state of Caucasia. While European immigrants such as Poles, Italians, Greeks, and Slavs who historically came to America during the late 19th and early 20th centuries did not arrive to the United States initially being viewed as "white," the dominant white society gradually accepted these various immigrants of different ethnicities as white, and therefore, American. This came at the expense of immigrants from Asia and South and Central America who were and continue to be summarily excluded from the dominant white society and are still not considered fully American despite their citizenship to the United States. They have and still continue to face discrimination from the white dominant class, as well as laws and government policies meant to otherize them. Palahniuk's novel should serve as an introductory text in a class dedicated to exploring the deep roots of white anxiety and nativism that have ebbed and flowed to various degrees but have been present, nonetheless, throughout all of American history. I would ask students to reflect back on the ways in which Palahniuk's novel seems positioned to address this history in a less confrontational, but not less critical, way.

The First to be Persecuted: Quakers, Scotch-Irish, and German Protestants during the Colonial Period

Despite proclaiming itself to be a haven for religious toleration, America has a long track record of abusing and persecuting immigrants, especially when they happen to be of a different religious persuasion or ethnic group. Puritans were the first Europeans to arrive and successfully settle in what has today become the United States of America. Shortly after, groups such as the Quakers arrived. This Society of Friends became one of the first groups to feel the wrath of the white dominant class in American society. Deemed heretical to the teachings of God by the Puritans, the Quakers were imprisoned, banished, and deported from the Puritanical "City on the Hill" in Massachusetts. Their books were burned, and most of their property was confiscated (Ward 16). Quakers were tortured, maimed, and even executed for their radical and unholy beliefs, as the Puritans thought them to be eroding their community.

The Quakers ultimately settled in their colony of supposed religious tolerance in Pennsylvania, where they were assimilated, and the next groups to replace the Quakers as an immediate threat to the dominant white class were the German and Scotch-Irish Protestants. It was in Pennsylvania during the early 18th century that the early iterations of "race suicide" began to stir in America and that the dominant white class would be overthrown by an influx of lesser and foreign peoples. The Germans and Scotch-Irish first started migrating to the colonies in large numbers during the early 18th century. One colonial leader, Patrick Gordon, warned the colony of Pennsylvania that their "peace and security" were being "endangered" by a great "numbers of strangers…who being ignorant of our language and laws, and settling in a body together, make…a distinct people from his Majesties subjects" (Glatfelter 6). Benjamin Franklin shared the sentiment of Gordon and stated that these newly arrived Germans were swarming the colony and threatening to "establish their language and manners to the exclusion of ours" (Glatfelter 6). And, if Franklin showed a distaste for the Germans who were arriving in Pennsylvania, his feelings towards the Scotch-Irish "amounted to hatred" (Kenny 174). He and several of his contemporaries referred to the Scotch-Irish as the "most flagitious banditti upon Earth" and presumed them to be disease-riddled criminals, with Franklin saying, "the Small Pox spreads" where the Scotch-Irish settle (Dickson 84). Grappling with this deep-seated ideology of exclusion, white supremacy, and othering that seems to come to a head in Palahniuk's *Adjustment Day* would begin with having students write about and then discuss in small groups a less rose-colored-glass version of American icons like Franklin and how his individual prejudices can be seen policy. The Pennsylvania colonial legislature put forward several laws aimed at curbing Scotch-Irish immigration into the colony, but ultimately decided against such measures. The reason, however, was not because the Quaker government suddenly decided the Scotch-Irish and Germans would be beneficial additions to their society, but rather that once these immigrants arrived, they could be pushed to the edges of the colonial frontier to serve as a human wall to protect those living in Philadelphia from the Indian incursions.

Historian Patrick Griffin argues that the Pennsylvania government made specific efforts to have the Germans and Scotch-Irish immigrants settle further westward in the colony to "provide a sound buffer to western Indians...to protect the east of the colony...and safeguard the colony's claim to lands further west" (162). Just as the leaders of Palahniuk's Caucasia pushed non-whites and those it viewed as "other" out of its society, so too did the dominant white class in colonial Pennsylvania push the German and Scotch-Irish immigrants out of Philadelphia to the most dangerous fringes of the colony in hopes of keeping them segregated from the larger community. When teaching a college course on nativism and white supremacy, it is important to highlight to students the roots of anti-immigrant sentiment and the otherizing of new arrivals to the United States as a common and recurrent American practice. The dominant white class used the same types of arguments during the 18th and 19th centuries against the Germans and Scotch-Irish that white nationalists and nativists use today, arguing that these immigrants come from a different culture with strange languages and customs and odd religious beliefs inconsistent and incompatible with American values. As a result, the white dominant class felt and still feels an obligation to try to keep these newcomers from arriving en masse, as they believe this cultural mixing will certainly dilute and deteriorate the American populace and its systems of power.

The Turning of the Tables: German and Scotch-Irish Protestants' Persecution of Catholics during the 19th Century

Yet another recurrent theme that must be pointed out when teaching students about the evolution of nativism and white supremacy in America is the cyclical concept of the former oppressed becoming the oppressors. I would start a discussion about this topic by having students work in small groups to identify instances of this dynamic in the novel and then challenge them to link the fiction examples to those they have encountered throughout American immigration history from their textbook. The immigrant groups once seen as the other eventually assimilate into the white dominant class, and as a rite of passage, they lead the nativist charge against the new group of arrivals who, they argue, are unassimilable to the American way of life. So, just as with the Quakers, over time, the Scotch-Irish and Germans were gradually taken in by the white dominant class as a new and dangerous group replaced them as public enemy number one: Irish and German Catholics. This papal threat to the white dominant class led to anti-Catholic sentiment gaining strength during the 1830s and 1840s, as well as the rise of the Know Nothings of the 1850s. The Know Nothings formed as a result of the influx of Catholics coming into the country during the previous two decades. The movement began as a conglomeration of secret nativist societies, who when asked about their movement, responded that they "knew nothing" about it, for as members of the oath-bound group, they were sworn to secrecy. The Know Nothing Party called out Catholics as mindless drones of the Pope who had no allegiance to their newfound home. The Know Nothings called for a 21-year naturalization period for all immigrants, who, until being fully naturalized would not be granted a number of rights, including voting and some property rights. They also refused to vote any Catholics into the elected office for fear of their loyalty to the Pope. This movement gained tremendous power by the mid-1850s, and the nativist group made up about one-third of the voting population (Anbinder 121; 99).

And although the native-born population of British ancestry certainly made up a large portion of the movement, it was the previously denigrated Scotch-Irish and German Protestants who led the charge against the new arrivals. Nativist groups like the Orange Orders of the 1830s were organizations comprised of Scotch-Irish Presbyterians and other Irish Protestants and were popular across the Northeast until the order was dissolved in 1836. According to Kevin Kenny, in the 1830s, "the Scotch-Irish used their Orange societies for nativist purposes and joined organizations like the American Protestant Association (which they dominated) in large numbers," during the 1840s and 1850s (81). As a result of this organization disbanding, the Scotch-Irish looked to join the above organizations in opposition to the new Catholic contingency.

Historian Lindsay Flewelling agrees with Kenny and asserts that the "Scotch-Irish were closely associated with the Know-Nothings, as well as other nativist organizations such as the American Protestant Association, [and] the Order of United Americans" (87). Tyler Anbinder, a scholar of immigration history and nativism, also asserts that the American Presbyterian community, a large majority of whom were of Scotch-Irish descent, "praised the Order" (Anbinder 49). However, the Know Nothings and the like-minded organizations sympathetic to the party ultimately fizzled out as the sectional within the movement over the slavery issue took precedence over the ethno-religious conflicts that propelled the Know Nothings to power. The Scotch-Irish would continue their nativist persecution of Catholic immigrants in the less powerful Know Nothing-style group known as the American Protective Association of the 1890s, but that too would fade away within a decade of its rise in American politics.

From the 1880s to the 1920s, there was a great influx of immigrants from southern and eastern Europe, mostly of Catholic or Jewish religious backgrounds. German Americans, just like the Scotch-Irish, continued to engage in nativist attacks against these "new immigrants" of southeastern Europe. During the late 19th century, Americans of German descent were "well-represented" among both the leadership and the rank-and-file members of nativist organizations like the Patriotic Order Sons of America (POSA), and Junior Order of United American Mechanics (Kazal 237). According to historian Russell Kazal, those whose parents and grandparents were subjected to nativist attacks were now the perpetuators of nativism and xenophobia, and were among the staunchest advocates for immigration restriction. The local POSA paper in Philadelphia, *Camp News,* seemed to highlight this phenomenon in which older immigrants and their descendants saw themselves as distinct and superior to the newer arrivals, when it stated, "God bless their daddies if they were immigrants—they are the kind of immigrants we want…real Americans, and in just one generation they assimilated…but God save us from what we are getting now—close the gates" (Kazal 237). This example clearly highlights an important phenomenon in the study of nativism and white supremacy that instructors of courses on such topics must address. As immigrants settled and established themselves in America, one final step in being assimilated into the white dominant class was redirecting the nativist attacks once used against them to the newer immigrants now arriving onto American shores. This cyclical pattern of the oppressed becoming the oppressors is essential to understand how the white dominant culture uses white supremacy to alienate immigrants against one another, and how the white dominant culture, in exchange for acceptance into it, forces immigrants to accept its nativist beliefs. As students move from studying the late 19th to early 20th century, I would ask them to write a brief synopsis of the evolution of nativist ideology, its targets, and its assimilators. I anticipate, by this point in the course, many students would begin connecting both real-world, historical examples with fictionalized examples of this ideology in action in *Adjustment Day*.

How Irish Catholics Became White: Anti-Chinese Sentiment and the Nativism against Southeastern European Immigrants

This phenomenon of immigrants embracing "whiteness" as a requirement for becoming a full "American," to the detriment of newer immigrants and non-white members of American society, is perhaps most clearly exemplified in the case of Irish Americans. During the late 19th century in America, the formerly disparaged Irish Catholic population began making inroads with the white dominant class in the face of a new "other:" Asian and southeastern European immigrants. While the Irish Catholics were the boogeymen of the mid-19th century, an influx of immigrants from Poland, Hungary, Greece, and Italy to the American northeast and Japanese and Chinese immigrants settling in the West Coast from across the Pacific, allowed the Celts to slowly but surely work their way to becoming white, albeit still not yet fully a part of the ruling white class.

According to whiteness studies scholar David Roediger, prior to the Civil War, Irish Catholics were not viewed as white by the dominant Protestant class. However, Roediger points to the end of the Civil War as a turning point, because this is when blacks joined the free labor force to compete with whites. According to Roediger, to the detriment of African Americans, it was this stark comparison between the Irish laborer and the former slave that aided in the slow integration of the Irish into white society (Roediger 13). Roediger's theory also applies to the relationship between Irish and Chinese immigrants, with the relative whiteness of the Irish working to their advantage to the detriment of the non-white Chinese. Scholarship on Asian immigration, such as historian Moon-Ho Jung's *Coolies and Cane*, have highlighted the vague and indeterminate space that Asian immigrants and Asian Americans have historically occupied. Asians have upset the traditional binaries within American society of white versus black and alien versus citizen. According to Jung, Asian immigrants during the 19th century often represented something "between and beyond"—an alien and a citizen—, making them "an ideal noncitizen" in American society (Jung 223). In Palahniuk's *Adjustment Day*, Asian Americans continue to occupy this nebulous space, as they fail to fit into either Blacktopia or Caucasia, and as a result, the majority are forced to self-deport to other countries. But while scholars such as Jung argue that Asians found themselves in between whites and blacks, he makes clear that that the white dominant culture, including the some of the newly initiated members, such as the Irish, made it explicitly clear that Asians were not white.

This can be most clearly seen in the example of Denis Kearney and the Workingmen's Party of California. Kearney, an Irish immigrant who settled in California, founded the Workingmen's Party in the 1870s. The party was major mobilizing force in the creation of anti-Chinese laws, such as the Chinese Exclusion Act of 1882. Despite being a newly arrived immigrant himself, Kearney and his Irish allies attempted to gain the good graces of and form an alliance with the native-born white labor population in California, and America more broadly, to place the blame for all of their woes on Chinese labor and immigration. In his speeches, he spoke of "white labor" as a way of unifying the newly branded "white" Irish with their native-born white laborers against a Chinese "other" (Kearney and Knight). He appealed to a white unity that transcended the ethno-religious tensions of the past that previously placed his Irish Catholic brethren at odds with the white Protestant dominant class, arguing, "We don't meet here as Irish, English, Scotch, or Dutch, nor are we Catholics, Protestants, Atheists, or Infidels. Let there be no sect" (Urban 171).

But despite the efforts of Kearney and his fellow Irish anti-Chinese nativists, it was not until the beginning of the 20th century that Irish Catholics would become mostly assimilated into the dominant white culture. While their religion was still a sticking point for some nativists, most Protestant white Americans had accepted them into their ranks as race became a more important marker of being accepted into the dominant white culture than ethnicity or religion. Even the Second Ku Klux Klan, which prided itself for being a white, male, Protestant, gentile organization notorious for its anti-Catholic views, admitted, "a slight mixture of Celtic blood is valuable to the Anglo-Saxon race" (Evans 7). Being incorporated into the mainstream white culture, the Irish now had the power and the motivation to point to a new "other" in society that could be scapegoated. According to Roediger, "the now settled Irish-American population itself judged the newcomers...acting as on-the-ground arbiters of whether and how fast such a transition could occur. Irish-American foremen, for example, often picked out which of the immigrant workers who lined up seeking work would be paid and which would be jobless that day" (Roediger 326). Irish-American laborers and their native-born contemporaries began to use racialized terms like "guinea" and "hunky" to highlight the differences between them and their not-quite-yet white European co-workers from places like Italy, Poland, Hungary, Greece, and other countries in southeastern Europe. Roediger notes using terms like this towards these new immigrants was a way for these nativists to "deny him of his whiteness" as Irish workers sought to "bar Italians from working alongside them" (Roediger 328).

Organized labor, whose rank-in-file members and leadership were largely comprised of Irish and German Catholic immigrants, now considered to be the "old stock" immigrants from northwestern Europe, took an early stance supporting the restriction of immigration from China, southeastern Europe, and Latin America. A Jewish immigrant from Britain, Samuel Gompers of the American Federation of Labor, argued for the exclusion of Chinese immigration during the late 1800s and early 1900s, as he claimed that Chinese migrants threatened the "quality of American citizenship" (Fine and Tichenor 85). Likewise, in the 1880s, Terence Powderly, the son of Irish immigrants and the leader of the Knights of Labor, argued against the immigration of southern and eastern Europeans, claiming that they undermined the labor movement because of their willingness to live in squalor and their inability to assimilate into the American way of life. He claimed, "if it were possible to make good and useful citizens of these [Hungarian] men, I would never raise my voice against them, but that is impossible. He may be fit to work—so is a mule" (Asher 328). Samuel Gompers of the AFL was also "a steadfast opponent of Chinese immigration," as well as an opponent of "immigration from eastern and southern Europe," leading the charge among organized labor in support of immigration restriction from the 1880s to the end of his tenure as president in 1924.

In the years following World War I, Gompers also noted the influx of Mexican immigrants into the country and advocated the implementation of a literacy test requirement, an assessment already required of immigrants from outside the western hemisphere (Allerfeldt 17). After he left his role as the leader of the Knights of Labor, Powderly went on to serve as the nation's commissioner-general of immigration, where he attempted to further push forward his anti-immigrant agenda. He was opposed to immigration from southern and eastern Europe, but to him, according to historian Erika Lee, the greatest threat was that of Asian immigration. Powderly argued, "those sturdy men of Scotland, Germany, Ireland," were always welcome to immigrate to America, while he condemned the "advancing hordes and whores who seek our shores" from Japan and China (Lee 65). This use of explicitly sexual language, highlights the historical trend in America in which nativists often associated Chinese, Japanese, and South Asians with sexual depravity, while at the same time, the white dominant culture engaged in a fetishization of Asian women. According to Erika Lee and Judy Yung, two of the foremost scholars on Asian immigration history, Chinese and Japanese women who arrived at the gates of Angel Island, the major port of entry for Asian immigrants during the early 20th century, were often turned away at higher rates than European women because of the stereotype that they were sexually immoral and were suspected of being prostitutes (Lee and Yung 81). Even today, Asian women continue to be fetishized in American culture, and this fetishization has resulted in the high rates of the sex trafficking of Asian women in the United States. Another result of this link between Asians and sexual depravity is white violence against Asian women, such as the 2021 mass killing by a white man of five Asian women linked to sex work in Atlanta, Georgia. The killer blamed these Asian women as being vessels of his perverse and immoral sexual desires and felt that killing them was the only way to remedy his own sexual immorality (Lenthang).

Aside from the links to sexual immorality, the white dominant culure often used the language of disease to refer to new immigrants, as they were metaphorically infecting the American people and American values with their foreign and inferior cultures. The Chinese, according to Terence Powderly, were a "contamination" and an "influence...wholly bad" for the American way of life (Yang 22). His rationale was one of racial purity and cultural homogeneity, arguing, "I am an American, and I believe that self-preservation is the first law of nations as well as nature" (Lee 65). Although leaders like Gompers and Powderly were first and second-generation immigrants themselves, they had no trouble with the idea of "closing the gates" behind them to immigrants of different ethnic and racial backgrounds that they viewed as unassimilable and a threat to America's values and demographic composition. This idea of the newer immigrants arriving being unassimilable, while previous immigrants were more willing to become "American" is still present in the Trump Era and makes including a work of fiction, like Palahniuk's *Adjustment Day*, essential for the way it can illustrate the persistence of trends that can be traced back through the nation's history and because its classification as fiction will more likely be disarming to those unconsciously sympathetic to nativist views or resistant to any assessment of American history that complicates narratives of steady, consistent progress toward justice and American exceptionalism. This can be seen in a 2019 survey in which a majority of Republicans viewed immigrants as a burden to the country by taking "jobs, healthcare, and housing," as well as a posing a threat whose increased presence in the United States could "risk losing our identity as a nation" (Relman). Furthermore, during class discussion, students could connect the nativism of the early 20th century with the way the modern GOP fixated on fomenting fear of immigrants as a part of election cycles with the 2018 migrant caravans from Central America and later weaponized it further in critiquing Biden's exit from Afghanistan. Trump himself, along with the right-wing punditry, seized on the ideas of immigrants tainting a pure, idealized America, and dedicated coverage and opening and closing monologues to how Afghani refugees would ruin rather than enhance the American communities into which they would be displaced. This negative perception of immigrants has ebbed and flowed over the course of American history, but the 1920s represented one of the highest peaks of xenophobia in the country.

By the middle of the Roaring Twenties, with the anti-immigrant sentiment at a fever pitch, and the Ku Klux Klan a major force in politics with millions of members nationwide, the gates of America were indeed closed. In 1924, President Calvin Coolidge signed the Johnson-Reed Immigration bill into law. The legislation, also known as the Quota Act or National Origins Act, was the most restrictive immigration bill in American history and greatly reduced immigration from southern and eastern Europe, as well as completely banning immigration from Asia. According to the new law, approximately 75 percent of all immigrants allowed to immigrate to America had to be from the British Isles, Ireland, and Germany, leaving the rest of Europe, Africa, and Latin America to make up the remaining 25 percent. This law remained in effect from 1924 until 1965, until it was repealed under the Johnson administration's Great Society reforms, which coincided with the major civil rights legislation. However, this half-century of serious crackdown on immigration allowed for a new "other" to emerge: non-whites.

During this period, the various ethnic immigrants of European heritage who were previously viewed as unassimilable slowly became considered to be white by dominant white class. While Asians, the Latin community, and African Americans were excluded by society, as happens in Palahniuk's *Adjustment Day*, there was a new but clear and "persistent association of whiteness with Americanism...these assumptions about racial difference were nourished by a newly assertive whiteness, born of the ardent desire of the "not-yet-white ethnics" (many of them Roman Catholic, second- and third-generation southern and eastern European immigrants) to move into the American mainstream. To be fully American was to be white" (Sugrue 60). These southern and eastern Europeans, previously excluded from the white dominant class, were now welcomed in while the gates were closed behind them to leave all non-whites out of the mainstream and pushed to the margins. This trend has continued to the present day, where Muslims and immigrants from Mexico and Central and South America have taken the place of Irish, Poles, Slavs, and Italians of the late 19th and early 20th century.

This unequal treatment along racial lines manifested itself in the imbalanced law enforcement response to the George Floyd protests in 2020 compared to the pro-Trump protests in 2020 and most notably on the events of the January 6, 2021 insurrection at the U.S. Capitol. While the George Floyd protests that broke out across the country in opposition to police violence and systemic racism were often met with an overwhelming show of force from law enforcement, several commentators noticed the discrepancy in comparison to the riot on January 6th by mostly white Trump supporters. According to the *New York Times*, "President Trump vowed to 'dominate' [the George Floyd] demonstrators, calling them 'extremists' and 'thugs,' while federal agents deployed tear gas and swept people into unmarked vans" (Dewan). Trump also threatened to deploy the "most vicious dogs, and most ominous weapons, I have ever seen" on these protestors (Dewan). The protests against police brutality in response to the killing of George Floyd were met with a seemingly militaristic police response as law enforcement donned riot gear and fought back against the demonstrators with bulletproof shields, batons, and tear gas.

In comparison, despite clear evidence of a potential coordinated efforts by white nationalists to undermine the democratic process of certifying the election results for then-president-elect Joe Biden in the days leading up to the January 6 insurrection, the Capitol police and associated law enforcement that were meant to protect American democracy from the rioters and insurrectionists were unprepared, and seemingly unmotivated to respond with force to the Trump-supporting mob. Footage from the insurrection showed capitol police allowing the rioters to enter the Capitol, and when asked why they were not stopping the white nationalist mob, one officer replied, "We've just got to let them do their thing now" (Dewan). Based upon the vastly disparate responses of law enforcement between these two instances, it seems clear that race plays a key role in how the government responds to civil unrest in America, and this is not something with which students are always comfortable articulating. However, from a pedagogical standpoint, having students both acknowledge observable fact and Palahniuk's poignant fiction, it can make some of these discussions feel safer and less like an indictment or betrayal of American history that students had likely previously encountered since they learn about Columbus sailing the ocean blue in Kindergarten.

In *Adjustment Day*, Palahniuk highlights the phenomenon of immigrants and their descendants from places like Germany and Northern Ireland as being the largest purveyors of nativism and prejudice. One particular scene from the book is told from the perspective of Miss Josephine, an old white woman whose former plantation has been seized by African Americans with the creation of Blacktopia in the American South. She knew who was to blame for the coup that left her dispossessed. According to Miss Josephine, "this was clearly the work of the Jew, the Jew in league with the Papist," who surreptitiously ripped away "the region's Scotch-Irish of their ancient birthright" (Palahniuk 150). She continued on by stating that the country truly began to go downhill just over a century prior, as it was in the 1890s that a "flood of immigrants from the Baltic region that conditions destabilized" (Palahniuk 152).

While nativism remained relatively dormant during the middle of the 20th century, as the foreign policy of the Cold War overshadowed issues like immigration, xenophobic sentiments have re-emerged with non-white immigrants as the new scapegoats. Over the past 30 years, nativism and white nationalism have been on the rise. Starting with increased white anxiety over Mexican immigration into the United States during the 1990s, the situation worsened with the Islamophobia of post 9/11 America. Over the past few years, nativism and white nationalism have reached new heights due to Donald Trump's strongly anti-immigrant rhetoric and subsequent policies during his administration and after. His words and actions have emboldened white nationalists and white supremacists around the country to the point that right-wing news outlets and conservative politicians have shifted from dog whistles to explicitly racist and white supremacist language. Fox News host Tucker Carlson claimed that allowing people from third-world countries into America "makes our own country poorer and dirtier and more divided" (Wemple). Fox's Laura Ingraham echoed these sentiments arguing,

> In some parts of the country, it does seem like the America that we know and love doesn't exist any more. Massive demographic changes have been hoisted upon the American people. And they're changes that none of us ever voted for and most of us don't like. From Virginia, to California, we see stark examples of how radically in some ways the country has changed. (Bump)

Comments like these from Fox News and from conservative politicians, as well as the white nationalist rallies in places like Charlottesville make it very clear that what many members of the dominant white class in America want is a Caucasia. With Islamophobic and xenophobic politicians like Congresswoman Marjorie Taylor Greene in the ascendancy of the Republican Party, it seems unlikely that non-white immigrants and Americans will be fully accepted by the dominant white class in the near future. Palahniuk expertly dissects the American fear of the "other" and how the white dominant class works tireless to undermine and scapegoat them. His forward-thinking and the prescience of his dystopian predictions contained in *Adjustment Day*, some of which have come true in the era of Trump and in light of the January 6 insurrection, highlight Palahniuk's acute understanding of American history, in which the white dominant class seeks to assert itself at the expense of all those who it believes do not fit into it. While the history of this phenomenon is well-documented through the numerous waves of xenophobia and racism recurring throughout the existence of the United States, despite the persistent denials of such nativism and white supremacy, his works of fiction, such as *Adjustment Day*, are elevated in their value in and out of the classroom beyond the repeated claims about its absurdity and invocation of shock value. Works of fiction, such as Palahniuk's *Adjustment Day* can be a useful tool for instructors in the field of English, as well as seemingly unrelated fields like history and political science, to highlight problematic ideologies like nativism and white supremacy, while helping students understand the consequences of these harmful belief systems. They can foster discussion, be addressed through short, in-class writing, and even contribute to original undergraduate and graduate research. Let us just hope that Palahniuk's dystopia and Richard Spencer's dream of a white ethnostate don't come true, as we find it doesn't end well for a white America that no longer has anyone but itself to blame for its own dysfunction.

Works Cited

Allerfeldt, Kristofer. "'And We Got Here First': Albert Johnson, National Origins and Self-Interest in the Immigration Debate of the 1920s." *Journal of Contemporary History*, vol. 45, no. 1, Sage Publications, 2010, pp. 7–26.

Anbinder, Tyler. *Nativism and Slavery: the Northern Know Nothings and the Politics of the 1850's*. Oxford UP, 1992.

Asher, Robert. "Union Nativism and the Immigrant Response." *Labor History*, vol. 23, no. 3, Summer 1982, p. 325.

Bump, Philip. "Laura Ingraham's Immigration Comments are Different Words for the same Trump-era Rhetoric." *Washington Post*. August 9, 2018.

Dewan, Shaila. "Police Response to Capitol Mob is Striking Contrast to Protests after George Floyd Killing." *New York Times*, 6 Jan. 2021. https://www.nytimes.com/2021/01/06/us/politics/capitol-george-floyd-dc-protests.html.

Dickson, R. J. *Ulster Emigration to Colonial America: 1718-1775*. Routledge & Kegan Paul, 1966.

Evans, Hiram Wesley. *The Klan of Tomorrow*, The Knights of the Ku Klux Klan, 1924.

Fine, Janice, and Daniel J. Tichenor. "A Movement Wrestling: American Labor's Enduring Struggle with Immigration, 1866-2007." *Studies in American Political Development*, vol. 23, no. 1, 2009, pp. 84-113.

Glatfelter, Charles Henry. *The Pennsylvania Germans: a Brief Account of Their Influence on Pennsylvania*. Pennsylvania Historical Association, 2002.

Griffin, Patrick. *The People with No Name: Ireland's Ulster Scots, America's Scots Irish, and the Creation of a British Atlantic World, 1689-1764*. Core Textbook, Princeton UP, 2012.

Grinberg, Emannuella, and Eliott C. McLaughlin. "Against Its Wishes, Auburn Hosts White Nationalist Richard Spencer." *CNN*, Cable News Network, a Warner Media Company, 19 Apr. 2017, www.cnn.com/2017/04/18/politics/auburn-richard-spencer-protests.

Jacobson, Matthew Frye. *Barbarian Virtues: the United States Encounters Foreign Peoples at Home and Abroad, 1876-1917*. 1st ed., Hill and Wang, 2000.

Jacobson, Matthew Frye. *Whiteness of a Different Color: European Immigrants and the Alchemy of Race*. Harvard UP, 1998.

Kazal, Russell. *Becoming Old Stock: The Paradox of German-American Identity*. Princeton UP, 2004.

Kearney, Denis and H. L. Knight. "Appeal from California. The Chinese Invasion. Workingmen's Address." *Indianapolis Times*, February 28, 1878.

Kenny, Kevin. *Peaceable Kingdom Lost the Paxton Boys and the Destruction of William Penn's Holy Experiment.* Oxford University Press, 2009.

Jung, Moon-Ho. *Coolies and Cane: Race, Labor, and Sugar in the Age of Emancipation.* Johns Hopkins UP, 2006.

Lee, Erika, and Judy Yung. *Angel Island: Immigrant Gateway to America.* Oxford UP, 2010.

Lee, Erika. *At America's Gates: Chinese Immigration During the Exclusion Era, 1882-1943.* U of NC P, 2003.

Lenthang, Martha. "Atlanta Shooting and the Legacy of Misogyny and Racism Against Asian Women: Advocates are Calling for Conversations to Unravel Harmful Stereotypes." *ABC News,* 21 Mar. 2021, https://abcnews.go.com/US/atlanta-shooting-legacy-misogyny-racism-asian-women/story?id=76533776.

Palahniuk, Chuck. *Adjustment Day.* First edition. W.W. Norton & Company, 2018.

Relman, Eliza. "Republican Voters have Become More Xenophobic as Trump has Normalized Racist Rhetoric." *Business Insider,* 18 Jul. 2020, https://www.businessinsider.com/republican-voters-have-become-more-xenophobic-under-trump-2019-7.

Roediger, David R. *How Race Survived US History: from Settlement and Slavery to the Eclipse of Post-Racialism.* Verso, 2019.

Roediger, David R. *The Wages of Whiteness: Race and the Making of the American Working Class.* Rev. ed., Verso, 1999.

Sugrue, Thomas J. *The Origins of the Urban Crisis Race and Inequality in Postwar Detroit.* Princeton UP, 2014.

Urban, Andrew Theodore. "An Intimate World: Race, Migration, and Chinese and Irish Domestic Servants in the United States, 1850--1920." *University of Minnesota,* 2009.

Ward, Madeleine. "Transformative Faith and the Theological Response of the Quakers to the Boston Executions." *Quaker Studies,* vol. 21, no. 1, 2016, pp. 15-32.

Wemple, Erik. "Tucker Carlson said Immigration Makes America 'Dirtier.' So an Advertiser Took Action." *Washington Post.* December 15, 2018.

Yang, Michelle Murray. "From Yellow to Red: The Emergence of the Red Peril in U.S. Political and Media Discourse." *American Political Discourse on China,* 1st ed., vol. 1, Routledge, 2017, pp. 18–55.

Index

A

Adorno, Theodor, 33, 38, 40, 41
Adjustment Day, vii, ix, x, xiii, xiv, 32, 33, 43, 44, 45, 46, 47, 48, 125, 126, 128, 130, 133, 136, 137, 138, 139, 141
Alt-Right, 125
American Psycho, 10
Aristophanes, xii, 104, 105, 123
Atwood, Margaret, ix

B

Bain, Ken, ix, 4, 99
Biden, Joe, x, 44, 138
Bly, Robert, 17, 18
Booker, M. Keith, x, 52, 53, 54, 65
Brodentity, ix, 17, 19, 20, 21, 22, 23, 29

C

Choke, viii, xiv
Clark, Michael J., 22
Collado-Rodriguez, Francisco, viii, 9, 76, 77, 78, 80
Crime and Punishment, vi
Critical Race Theory, ix, 31, 32, 43, 44, 46, 47, 48

D

Daniels, Stormy, xii, xiii, 103, 106, 108, 114, 115, 116, 118, 119, 120, 123
Dworkin, Andrea, xii, 110

E

Easter Bunny, x, 56, 57, 63
Ellman, Lucy, 120, 121
Ellwanger, Adam, 45
Erickson, Erik, 22
"Expedition" (short story), 1, 6, 7, 8, 9

F

Fagan, Kate, 20
Fight Club, viii, ix, xiv, 2, 3, 4, 5, 6, 7, 8, 9, 10, 11, 12, 13, 14, 15, 17, 18, 19, 20, 22, 24, 25, 26, 28, 29, 30, 33, 34, 35, 36, 37, 38, 39, 41, 42, 43, 44, 46, 47, 52, 67, 76, 80, 86, 91, 96, 101
"Fight Club" (short story), x, 10, 34, 35, 36, 37
Fight Club 2, 1, 6, 7,8, 9, 12
Fight Club 3, viii, 14
Foucault, Michel, 33, 38, 39
Franklin, Benjamin, 126, 129, 130
Freud, Sigmund, 33, 41, 42
Friedan, Betty, 18, 26

G

#Gamergate, ix, 21
Gold, Stephen, 20, 29
Gooblar, David, 8, 11, 88, 89, 91
Gothic Loop, xi, 77, 86
"Guts", vii, xi, xii, 87, 88 90, 92, 93, 94, 95, 96, 97, 98, 100, 101

H

Haunted, xiv
Horkheimer, Max, 33, 38, 40, 41
Hume, Kathryn, ix, 9

I

Invisible Monsters, viii, xiv, 52

J

Jacobson, William Frye, 125, 128
Jefferys, Sheila, xii, 103, 106, 110, 112, 113, 120

K

Kavanaugh, Matt, 32
Keen, Sam, 17, 18
Keesey, Douglas, vi, vii, ix, xii, 2, 3, 14, 71, 72, 73, 75, 86, 88, 90, 93, 95, 100, 101, 109, 117, 120, 121
Key & Peele, ix, 26

L

Lang, James, ix, xii, 7, 11, 95
Lee, Terry, 20
Levy, Ariel, xii, 110, 111, 112
Lullaby, xi, 69, 70, 71, 72, 73, 74, 75, 76, 77, 78, 80, 81, 84, 85, 86
Lysistrata, xii, 104, 105, 106, 107, 112, 118, 122, 123

M

Make Something Up: Stories You Can't Unread, xii, 6, 110
Masculinity, 17, 18, 19, 20, 21, 24, 25, 28, 29
McCracken, David, ix, xii, 8, 72, 88, 99, 100, 103

#MeToo Movement, xii, xiii, 103
Milano, Alyssa, xii, 104, 105, 112, 118, 119, 121
Millett, Kate, 21
Mookerjee, Robin, ix, 9, 90
Mulan, ix, 17, 26, 27

N

Newman, Sandra, vi
"Not Chasing Amy" (essay), xii, 33, 91, 96, 97
Nugenix, 25

O

Old Man and the Sea, vi
Orenstein, Peggy, 18

P

Palahniuk, Chuck, v, vi, vii, viii, ix, x, xi, xii, xiii, xiv, 2, 3, 5, 6, 7, 8, 9, 11, 12, 13, 14, 15, 18, 19, 20, 22, 24, 25, 26, 27, 28, 29, 30, 31, 32, 33, 34, 35, 36, 37, 38, 39, 40, 42, 43, 44, 45, 46, 47, 48, 54, 55, 56, 57, 58, 59, 60, 61, 62, 63, 64, 66, 67, 69, 70, 71, 72, 73, 74, 75, 76, 77, 78, 80, 81, 82, 85, 86, 88, 90, 91, 92, 93, 94, 95, 96, 97, 98, 99, 100, 101, 105, 106, 107, 109, 110, 111, 115, 116, 117, 118, 119, 120, 121, 122, 125, 127, 128, 129, 130, 133, 136, 137, 138, 139, 140, 141
Peterson, Jordan, 11, 12
Post-Traumatic Stress Disorder (PTSD), xi, 78, 79, 85

R

Rant: An Oral History of Buster Casey, x, xiv, 49, 50, 54, 55, 56,

57, 58, 59, 60, 61, 62, 63, 64, 65, 66, 67
Recco, Rebecca, xii, 99
Riekki, Ron, 39
Ruden, Sara, 104, 105, 107

S

Santa Claus, x, 56, 57, 63, 64
Sartain, Jeffrey, 32
Savran, David, 22
#SexStrike, xii, 104, 122
Shakespeare, William, vi
Silverblatt, Michael, 90, 109
Snuff, xii, xiv, 96, 101, 103, 105, 106, 107, 108, 109, 110, 113, 115, 116, 117, 118, 120, 121, 122
Sousanis, Nick, 13
Spencer, Richard, xiii, 125, 127, 140
SportsClips, 24, 25
Steinem, Gloria, 18

T

Ta, Lynn, 22
The Handmaid's Tale, ix, 14, 92, 97
The Wasteland, vi
Tooth Fairy, x, 56, 57, 58, 63
Trauma narrative, xi, 70, 71, 75, 78
Trump, Donald, v, vii, x, xii, xiii, xiv, 10, 14, 44, 47, 48, 50, 51, 53, 103, 106, 114, 115, 119, 121, 123, 126, 127, 136, 137, 138, 139, 140, 141

U

Unflattening, 13

V

Vickroy, Laurie, 76, 80, 85

W

Warner, John, ix, 11, 13
Wilson, Waleisah, xii, 104, 112
Whiteness, 133, 134
White anxiety, xiv, 125
Wright, Jennifer, 21

www.ingramcontent.com/pod-product-compliance
Lightning Source LLC
Chambersburg PA
CBHW061451300426
44114CB00014B/1938